CAESAR'S INVASION OF BRITAIN

JULIUS CAESAR.

From the bust in the British Museum.

Elementary Classics

Caesar's
Invasion of Britain

Adapted for the Use of Beginners, with Notes,
Exercises, and Vocabularies, by

W. Welch, M.A.

AND

C. G. Duffield, M.A.

Formerly Headmaster, Maidstone Grammar School

WITH ILLUSTRATIONS

LONDON
MACMILLAN & CO LTD
NEW YORK · ST MARTIN'S PRESS
1965

First Edition printed 1884
Reprinted 1885, 1886, 1887, 1888, 1890, 1891, 1892
1894, 1895, 1897, 1898, 1900
With Illustrations 1901, 1902, 1904, 1905, 1906, 1907
1908 (*twice*), 1909, 1910, 1911, 1912, 1914 (*twice*)
1916, 1917, 1919 (*twice*), 1921 (*twice*), 1923, 1925, 1927
1930, 1933, 1937, 1942, 1950, 1953, 1958, 1962, 1965

MACMILLAN AND COMPANY LIMITED
St Martin's Street London WC 2
also Bombay Calcutta Madras Melbourne

THE MACMILLAN COMPANY OF CANADA LIMITED
70 Bond Street Toronto 2

ST MARTIN'S PRESS INC
175 Fifth Avenue New York 10 NY

PRINTED IN GREAT BRITAIN

PREFACE.

CAESAR'S 'Invasion of Britain' is intended as a first
Translation Book. The text, which has been taken
from Books IV. and V. of the Gallic War, has been
simplified as much as possible; the various construc-
tions being introduced gradually to the learner's
notice. On each construction will be found one or
more exercises and an explanation or rule.

An English vocabulary has been added at the
request of the Publishers, and the objection raised to
such a vocabulary in the Introduction to the Eutropius
has been overcome by giving a reference to the
chapter or vocabulary where the word occurs instead
of giving the Latin word itself.

CONTENTS.

LIST OF ILLUSTRATIONS.

The portrait, which has suffered from cleaning, but is undoubtedly ancient, represents Caesar in old age; he is inclined to baldness, and his cheeks are shrunken. We know that he is said to have worn a wreath to hide his baldness; and Suetonius also says that for the same purpose he combed his scanty hair forward, as we see it represented on this head.

Julius Caesar, who is described as CAESAR DICT-(ator) PERPETVO, is represented wearing a thick laurel wreath. This is one of the latest portraits executed during the Dictator's lifetime.

The types of this coin are, though it may seem incredible, merely a degradation of the types of the gold stater of Philip II. of Macedon. On the obverse, the remains of the laurel-wreath are visible; on the reverse the horse is practically all that remains of the two horses and chariot with charioteer. The rest is meaningless ornament invented by the fancy of the barbarian out of a type which, as it became more and more degraded by unintelligent copying, he more and more failed to understand.

Caesar (*Bell. Gall.* v. 12) says of the Britons: 'Utuntur aut aere aut nummo aureo aut taleis ferreis ad certum pondus examinatis pro nummo.' Since we have gold coins of the Britons dating back to a period long before Caesar's invasion—these coins can hardly be later than 100 B.C.—there is no reason for bracketing as spurious the words 'aut nummo aureo,' as some editors do. The words which should be bracketed are 'aut aere'; they have probably come in from the statement made below: 'aere utuntur importato.'

Relief from Pompeii.

The details of this *navis oneraria* are very clear. The aplustre ends in a goose-head (χηνίσκος), to which is fastened a flagstaff (στυλίς) with ensign. The steersman (*gubernator*) controls the steering-oar (*gubernaculum*). The crew are engaged in furling (*contrahere*) the sails; one of them is running up the shrouds, another is on the fore-stay; two are on the yard (*antenna*), which is spliced. An ensign also flies from the masthead. The figure-head is a head of Minerva or Roma in a helmet.

From a grave-stone at Bonn, of the first century after Christ. The ground is imaginary.

Pintaius the *signifer*, from whose grave-stone this illustration is taken, wears over his head and shoulders a skin, which covers the helmet of which the cheek-pieces are visible. Under his jerkin is a coat of mail (*lorica*), and under that a *tunica*. On his feet are toeless boots. He wears sword and dagger in belts which gird his waist. The *signum* is decorated with (beginning from the top) a wreath, cross-bar with pendants, metal disc, the eagle of Jupiter standing on a thunderbolt, crescent moon, etc.

From a relief in the Louvre, about the beginning of the
Christian era. The ground is imaginary.

The soldiers wear coats of mail (*lorica hamata*), not scale-armour, as suggested in the illustration, over their tunics, and carry short daggers. The shield of the one on the left has for device a winged thunderbolt.

From a relief at Verona of Imperial date.
The ground is imaginary.

This is the grave-stone of Q. Sertorius, a centurion of the Eleventh Legion, known as the 'Claudia pia fidelis.' He carries the wand (*vitis*) of office, and wears the *corona civica* of oak-leaves (little but the tie of this crown is visible in the illustration). Over his *tunica* he wears a coat of scale-armour (*lorica squamata*); his phalerae are fastened on the usual framework, and two *torques* hang from his neck. The circular object by his left hand is the pommel of his sword. He also wears greaves (*ocreae*) and boots (*caligae*), and carries his cloak (*sayum*).

Relief at Bonn, of Imperial period.

This is the grave-stone of one C. Marius. The deceased is armed with a six-sided shield and spear. The metal discs on the frame which covers his breast are *phalerae*, decorations (*dona militaria*) more or less corresponding to our war medals; we see them again on a larger scale at the bottom of the relief. The two bracelets represented at the side of the *phalerae* and

the two pairs of *torques* above the niche are further
decorations.

From the sea near Actium. In the British Museum.

This figure-head may possibly have belonged to one
of the smaller vessels engaged in the battle of Actium
(31 B.C.). It is known that Augustus owed his
success to the small *naves Liburnae.* The bust represents the goddess Roma, wearing a helmet and aegis.

*Roman silver coin (denarius) issued by the triumvir M. Antonius
in the East between 39 and 31 B.C. In the British Museum.*

The galley is proceeding to the right. The stern
carries an aplustre and small circular shield (not well
shown on this specimen); the stem runs up in the
form usual at this time. There are small cabins in
the forecastle and poop; from the former rises a
foremast carrying a pennon (?). The inscription is
ANT. AVG. III . VIR. R. P. C., *i.e.* 'Antonius augur
triumvir reipublicae constituendae.' On the reverse is
an *aquila* between two *signa* ornamented with discs.
The inscription is CHORTIVM PRAETORIARVM,
showing that the coin was struck for the payment of
the Praetorian Cohorts, or Guards. Note the form
CHORTIVM, which is not uncommon in Latin in-
scriptions.

From a relief on Trajan's Column, 113 A.D.

This figure represents one of a party engaged in
storming Sarmizegetusa, the Dacian capital. He
holds the sling, with the bolt in it, in his right hand.
The sling is a short one, and the left hand is apparently
not used in discharging it.

From a relief on the Column of Marcus Aurelius
(shortly after 169 A.D.).

This represents an attack on a German fortress, the
wall of which seems to be made of wattles. The
Romans approach *testudine facta, i.e.* placing their
shields close together and overlapping so that missiles
glide off, as they would off the back of a tortoise.
Torches, swords, a pot full of molten metal, stones,
spears, etc., are the missiles used by the defenders.

MAP FOR THE INVASION OF BRITAIN.

Modern names thus:— *Canterbury*
Probable line of voyage & march thus:------

Walker & Boutall sc.

INTRODUCTION.

JULIUS CAESAR IN BRITAIN.

THE transactions recorded in this book should be of
the highest importance to Englishmen, for, however
transient in their effects, they mark the dawn of the
history of our island. Before the year 55 B.C., Britain
was a *terra incognita* to the ancient world at Rome.
The first mention of the island by any Roman writer
is found only in the second book of Caesar's Gallic
War, and even then he knew next to nothing about
it. In 55 B.C. all Gaul lay prostrate at the feet
of the conqueror; one by one the tribes had suc-
cumbed, and although they were only waiting an
opportunity to strike again for freedom, the advancing legions had carried their victorious arms to the
northern sea-coast of Gaul. Suddenly a new danger
arose; the barbarous hordes of Germany poured
across the Rhine upon their helpless neighbours;
Caesar was summoned hastily from Rome and hurry-
ing across the wintry passes of the Alps he met the
invader near the junction of the Mosa and the Rhenus,

and after a most determined battle nearly annihilated two entire tribes. It was at this time that the invasion of Britain was determined upon. If Gaul were to be preserved as a Roman dependency, it must be delivered from foreign foe and foreign ally alike. A severe example had just been made of one of the former, which would intimidate the rest for some time to come. But this was not enough. Caesar reflected that, in the conflict with the Veneti the year before, when all the maritime tribes had sent help against him, a fleet had sailed in from the direction of the white cliffs that lay far out on the horizon, and had joined the Venetian League. This was enough. If the security of his Gallic conquests was to be preserved, this mysterious ally from across the sea must be taught the power of the Roman arms. An unconquered people, so close at hand, would offer an example of independence highly dangerous to the peace of Gaul. At all hazards, therefore, the Britons must be silenced. Caesar took up his quarters on the coast of the Morini, who provided him with information and assistance. Volusenus, a Roman officer, was sent to reconnoitre the opposite coast. Commius, chief of the Atrebates, was commissioned to precede the Romans and impress upon the Britons the advisability of an alliance or submission to the Roman power. The autumn was advancing; little way could be made this year, an expedition would not be thrown away however, and so upon the evening of the 26th of August, B.C. 55, two divisions, consisting of two legions and a few hundred cavalry, were arranged to sail from two ports in the country of the Morini. Caesar with his legions made a favourable passage, and in a few hours was under the Dover cliffs where the hostile tribesmen were gathered to repel the invader. To land here was impracticable, and the other squadron of ships had not yet arrived. Accordingly Caesar drifted up seven or eight miles with the tide and arrived off the flat beach of Deal. The Britons were on the alert, and rushed into the waves to bar his landing. A hard fight followed; the Britons fought stubbornly; the ships of war drawn up on the flanks poured volley after volley of darts upon them; the Britons were dazed but unbeaten, when an ensign of the 10th legion, calling on his comrades to follow, dashed into the water at their head and drove back the Britons upon the shore. Their courage failed and they fled. A fortified camp was constructed on the shore, and the Britons at once began to send embassies with overtures of peace. Meantime Caesar's other detachment had been less fortunate; detained in harbour for four days after the first had sailed, they started at last to join the main body of ships. They were no sooner sighted from the camp on shore than a strong gale sprang up from the east and beat them down channel; some succeeded, however, in making the coast of Gaul in safety, while others were driven down the coast of Britain. This storm nearly proved fatal to the Romans on shore. The war vessels drawn upon the beach were shattered by the breakers, the transports at anchor were dragged from their moorings and dashed upon the coast. Nor was this the only misadventure. About the same time the Britons made an attack upon the seventh legion, which had been sent upon a foraging expedition, but as it was not out of communication with the camp, they were repulsed. Not a moment was to be lost. The shattered vessels were repaired, and in view of the coming stormy season, offers of submission made by the barbarians were accepted, and Caesar set sail for Gaul without delay.

In the spring of B.C. 54, preparations were completed for a descent upon Britain with a much larger force. Six hundred transports, with five legions and the pick of the Gallic cavalry on board, sailed from Portus Itius and, without casualty, landed at the same spot as in the preceding summer. A naval station was constructed on the shore, and a permanent camp pitched at some distance inland without the slightest opposition. It was not until he arrived at the banks of the little river Stour that he met with any bar to his progress, and even then the Britons at once fell back upon their entrenchment, a clearing in a neighbouring wood, where they were dislodged by the seventh legion. Next day news came from Q. Atrius, who had been left behind on shore to guard the naval station, that a storm on the previous night had again wrought havoc amongst the fleet. To prevent similar destruction for the future, Caesar determined to beach the remainder of the fleet and fortify the vessels with a camp on the shore, a task costing his men ten days of ceaseless labour. Meanwhile the British tribes had rallied under Cassivellaunus, a chief of the Catuvelauni, and were prepared to dispute his advance at the river Stour. The fleet secured, Caesar rejoined his legions, and a most determined battle ensued. Again and again the Britons in their war-chariots dashed at the Roman lines, but they never gave way, while the former lost the flower of their warriors. The Roman arms won the day, and never again was Caesar met in the open field. In spite of numerous irregular skirmishes he pushed on boldly, and arrived at the banks of the Thames, at a spot eighty miles from the sea. Here he found a ford, but the opposite bank was fortified with stakes driven into it. and the enemy were waiting to receive him. It is almost impossible to say where this spot was, but a long cherished tradition has fixed upon Cowey Stakes—an old ford on the river near the junction of the Wey with the Thames —as the place where Caesar crossed. No real opposition was encountered here, the Romans forded the river easily, carrying all before them, and Caesar marched straight on Verulamium, the stronghold of Cassivellaunus. On his way he received the submission of the Trinobantes, over whom Cassivellaunus had usurped authority, as well as that of several other tribes, and Cassivellaunus had to meet the invaders with only a handful of followers sheltered in the morasses and thickets in which his capital lay. Here he held out for a time ; he urged the Britons of Cantium to attack the Roman camp on the shore, which they did without success. His last chance was gone, and he surrendered to the Romans on hearing of the failure of the attack.

Caesar was now in haste to return to Gaul. News had reached him that a spirit of rebellion was abroad there, and to quell it his legions must return. After exacting tribute and hostages from Cassivellaunus he re-embarked his legions and sailed away to Gaul, never to return. Thus ended a most fruitless expedition. The Britons were beaten, yet no territory was added to the Roman power; not a single garrison was left behind ; no British wealth was poured into the treasury at Rome ; no train of captive Britons trod the Sacra Via before the conqueror's chariot. Much bravery and determination, many lives, and a large number of vessels had been thrown away upon it with this result. As Tacitus says in his 'Agricola,'

Contemporary British Coin.
From the British Museum.

Portrait of Julius Caesar on a Coin of Buca.

Navis Oneraria. (Schreiber-Anderson.)

54°   4°   2°   0°   2°   4°   54°

? Mona

BRITANNIA

Cenimagni

Verulamium
Cassio Trinobantes
Bibroci
Ancalites Londinium Tamesis
Segontiaci Cantii Portus
Dubris
Portus Itius

Damnonii

Vectis

ATREBATES

MORINI

Rhenus

Sequana
Parisii
Matrona

GALLIA

VENETI

English Miles

0   50   100   150

Typo. Etching Co. SG.

Caesar "rather showed Britain to posterity than handed it down to them as a conquest." It was not until nearly a hundred years later, in the reign of the Emperor Claudius (A.D. 43 and 44), that any part of Britain was annexed to the Roman empire.

(The localities mentioned above are disputed by various writers; many places contend for the honour of Caesar's landing-place, but the views of Mr. George Long on such matters have been adopted, and to him the editors are indebted for help in other parts of the book.)

DIRECTIONS FOR TRANSLATING.

1. Pick out the finite verb (the **predicate**) and find out its voice, mood, tense, number, and person.

2. Find the **subject** or subjects with which it agrees. Translate.

3. If the verb is incomplete, find the **object** or **completion**. Translate.

4. See if the **subject** is **enlarged** by any of the methods mentioned below ; if it is, translate, taking the **enlargements** with the subject.

5. See if the **object** is **enlarged** ; if it is, translate, taking the **enlargements** with the object.

6. Take the **extensions of the predicate**. Translate.

7. Translate finally, putting in the introductory conjunctions or other words not yet taken.

The **subject** may be

1. A noun.
2. A pronoun (perhaps understood in the verb).
3. An adjective.
4. An infinitive mood.
5. A phrase.

The **subject** may be **enlarged** by

1. An adjective or participle.
2. An noun in apposition.
3. A noun in the genitive case.
4. A relative clause.
5. A participial phrase.

The **object** or **completion** may consist of a phrase or of any of the parts of speech which can form a **subject**.

The **object** may be enlarged in the same way as the **subject**.

The **predicate** may be extended by

1. Adverb.
2. Ablative case.
3. Preposition and its case.
4. Adverbial sentence.

RULES OF AGREEMENT.

1. The verb agrees with its subject in number and person (and gender in the compound tenses).

2. The adjective agrees with its substantive in gender, number, and case.

3. The relative agrees with its antecedent in gender and number ; for case it looks to its own verb.

PARSING.

1. *Verb.* Person, number, tense, mood, and voice, from ———— (give the parts). Agrees with ————, its subject.

2. *Noun.* Case, number, and gender, from ————, of the ———— declension. Give the reason for the case.

3. *Adjective.* Case, number, and gender, from ———— and is declined like ————. It agrees with its substantive ————. Give the comparative and superlative.

4. *Relative.* Case, number, and gender, from ————. It agrees with its antecedent ————. Give the reason for the case.

ROMAN STANDARD-BEARER.

*From a Grave-Stone at Bonn; of the First
Century A.D.*

ROMAN LEGIONARIES.

*From a Relief in the Louvre; about the beginning
of the Christian Era.*

ROMAN CENTURION.
From a Relief at Verona of Imperial Date:

CAESAR'S INVASION OF BRITAIN.

1. Jam exigua pars aestatis reliqua fuit:

Caesar tamen in Britanniam proficisci statuit:

Caesar makes inqui-
ries about Britain.

Britanni in omnibus fere Gallicis bellis auxilium
hostibus nostris subministraverant.

2. Sed primo genus hominum, loca, portus, aditus 5
cognoscere statuit:

haec omnia fere Gallis erant incognita.

Nemo enim, praeter mercatores, illo adiit:

neque iis ipsis quidquam praeter oram maritimam 10
notum est.

3. Itaque mercatores ad se convocat:

Sed ea quae maxime cognoscere volebat, insulae
magnitudinem, incolarum genus, usum belli, reperire
non poterat. 15

C. Volusenum cum navi longâ praemittit:

ipse autem cum omnibus suis copiis
in Morinos proficiscitur:

His preparations.

inde erat brevissimus in Britanniam trajectus.

4. Huc naves undique venire jubet: 20

et classem, quam ad Veneticum bellum effecerat, convenire jubet.

Interim consilium ejus per mercatores ad Britannos perlatum est :

25   legati ab insulae civitatibus ad eum veniunt :

obsides dare et imperio populi Romani obtemperare volunt.

5. Caesar, liberaliter pollicitus, eos domum remittit.

Commium autem unà cum iis mittit :

30   hunc Caesar regem constituerat :

hujus virtutem et consilium probabat :

Commius enim Caesari fidelis esse videbatur :

et ejus auctoritas in his regionibus magna habebatur.

Volusenus autem neque e navi egredi neque se

35 barbaris committere audet.

Itaque quinto die ad Caesarem redit :

et, quae viderit, renuntiat.

<small>Help given him by the Morini.</small>   **6**. Caesar in his locis moratur : et naves parat :

40   Legati ex magnâ parte Morinorum ad eum veniunt :

de superioris temporis consilio se excusant :

olim enim bellum populo Romano fecerant.

Hoc Caesari esse opportunum videbatur :

nam neque post tergum hostem relinquere volebat,

45   neque facultatem belli gerendi propter anni tempus habebat.

His magnum numerum obsidum imperat, et eos in fidem recipit.

Trooper. Schreiber-Anderson.)

Figure-head of Galley   From original in the British Museum.

Warship and Standards.   Coin of M. Antonius.

7. Naves circiter octoginta onerarias cogit:

hae satis esse numero ei videbantur : 50

sed praeter eas quasdam naves longas habebat :

has quaestori, legatis praefectisque distribuit.

Huc accedebant duodeviginti onerariae naves,

quae ex eo loco ab millibus passuum octo vento

tenebantur : 55

has equitibus distribuit.

Publium Sulpicium Rufum legatum cum praesidio

portum tenere jussit.

8. Mox tempestatem ad navigationem idoneam

nactus est : 60

tum naves tertiâ fere vigiliâ solvit :

equitesque in ulteriorem portum progredi, et naves

conscendere, et se sequi jussit.

Ipse autem horâ circiter diei quartâ cum primis

navibus Britanniam attigit : 65

et ibi armatas hostium copias in omnibus collibus

expositas conspexit.

9. Haec erat loci natura :

mare angustis montibus continebatur :

telum ex locis superioribus in litus adigi pote- 70

rat.

Hic nequaquam idoneus locus esse videbatur :

et ad nonam horam reliquas naves in ancoris

exspectabat.

Interim legatos tribunosque militum convocat, et eos 75

hortatur.

Postea et ventum et aestum uno tempore secundum nanciscitur :

signum dedit : ancorae sublatae sunt.

80 **10.** Tum circiter millia passuum septem ab eo loco progressus est,

et naves in aperto ac plano litore constituit.

At barbari consilium Romanorum cognoscunt :

85 The Britons show fight.   equitatum et essedarios praemittunt: hoc plerumque genere militiae in proeliis uti consuescunt.

Itaque subsecuti reliquis copiis nostros e navibus egredi prohibent.

11. Erat ob has causas summa difficultas :

90 naves propter magnitudinem nisi in alto constitui non poterant :

militibus nostris loca ignota erant :

manus eorum impeditae erant :

ipsi magno et gravi onere armorum oppressi erant.

95 Hostes autem aut ex arido, aut paulum in aquam progressi, audacter tela conjecerunt :

et equos insuefactos incitaverunt.

12. Quibus rebus nostri perterriti, atque hujus omnino generis pugnae imperiti, non solitâ alacritate utebantur.

100 The Britons receive a check. Pluck of a Roman standard-bearer.   Quod ubi Caesar animadvertit, naves longas paulum removeri ab onerariis navibus, et remis incitari, et ad latus apertum hostium constitui, atque inde fundis, sagittis, tormentis hostes propelli ac summoveri jus

sit : (navium longarum et species erat barbaris inusi- 105
tatior et motus ad usum expeditior).

Quae res magno usui nostris fuit.

Nam barbari, et navium figurâ et remorum motu
et inusitato genere tormentorum permoti, constiterunt
ac paulum modo pedem rettulerunt. 110

13. Atque nostris militibus cunctantibus, maxime
propter altitudinem maris, quidam decimae legionis
aquilifer, contestatus deos, ut ea res legioni feliciter
eveniret: *"Desilite,"* inquit, *"milites, nisi vultis aquilam
hostibus prodere: ego certe meum reipublicae atque imperatori* 115
officium praestitero." Mox se ex navi projecit atque in
hostes aquilam ferre coepit. Tum nostri, tantum
dedecus metuentes, universi ex navi desiluerunt. Hos
item ex proximis navibus ubi conspexerant, subsecuti
hostibus adpropinquârunt. 120

14. Pugnatum est ab utrisque acriter. Nostri tamen
magnopere perturbabantur : nam ne- Engagement on the
que ordines servare neque firmiter in- beach. Victory of
the Romans.
sistere, neque signa subsequi poterant, atque alius aliâ
ex navi, quibuscumque signis occurrerat, se aggrega- 125
bat. Hostes vero, notis omnibus vadis, ubi ex litore
aliquos singulares ex navi egredientes conspexerant,
equos incitabant: nostros impeditos adoriebantur :
plures paucos circumsistebant: alii ab latere aperto in
universos tela conjiciebant. 15. Quod ubi viderat 130
Caesar, scaphas longarum navium, item speculatoria
navigia a militibus compleri jussit, et iis, quos laborantes

conspexerat, subsidia submittebat.   Nostri ubi in
arido constiterunt, suis omnibus consecutis, in hostes
135 impetum fecerunt atque eos in fugam dederunt: neque
longius prosequi potuerunt, quod equites cursum tenere
atque insulam capere non potuerant.   Hoc unum ad
pristinam fortunam Caesari defuit.

  16. Hostes, proelio superati, simul atque se ex fugâ

140 The Britons sue for   receperunt, statim ad Caesarem legatos
peace and restore
Commius,the envoy,   de pace miserunt : promittunt se ob-
whom they held in
custody.   sides daturos esse, et Caesaris mandata
effecturos.   Unà cum his legatis Commius Atrebas
venit, qui a Caesare in Britanniam antea praemissus
145 erat.   Hunc Britanni, e navi egressum, quum ad eos
oratoris modo Caesaris mandata deferret, comprehend-
erant atque in vincula conjecerant.   **17.** Tum proelio
facto, remiserunt et ejus rei culpam in multitudinem
contulerunt, et ut ignosceretur propter imprudentiam
150 petiverunt.   Caesar questus est, quod bellum sine causâ
intulissent; dixit se ignoscere imprudentiae obsidesque
imperavit : quorum illi partem statim dederunt, partem ex longinquioribus locis arcessitam se daturos
paucis diebus dixerunt.   Interea suos remigrare in
155 agros jusserunt, principesque undique convenire, et se
civitatesque suas Caesari commendare coeperunt.

Destruction of the   **18.** Pace confirmatâ, naves duode-
Roman fleet by a
storm.   viginti, quae equites sustulerant, ex
superiore portu leni vento solverunt.   Quae quum
160 appropinquarent Britanniae et ex castris viderentur

magna tempestas subitò coorta est : neque ulla navis
cursum tenere poterat ; sed aliae eodem, unde erant
profectae, referebantur, aliae ad inferiorem partem
insulae, quae est propius solis occasum, magno sui cum
periculo dejiciebantur : quae tamen, ancoris jactis, 165
fluctibus complebantur: itaque necessariò adversâ nocte
in altum provectae continentem petiverunt. Eâdem
nocte accidit, ut esset luna plena, qui dies maritimos
aestus maximos in Oceano efficere consuevit ; nos-
trisque id erat incognitum. 19. Ita uno tempore et 170
longas naves, quibus Caesar exercitum transportaverat,
quasque in aridum subduxerat, aestus complebat, et
onerarias, quae ad ancoras erant deligatae, tempestas
afflictabat ; neque ulla nostris facultas aut administrandi aut auxiliandi dabatur. Complures naves 175
fractae sunt ; reliquae, funibus, ancoris, reliquisque
armamentis amissis, erant ad navigandum inutiles :
itaque magna totius exercitûs perturbatio facta est.
Neque enim naves erant aliae, quibus reportari possent, et omnia, quibus naves refici possent, deerant : et 180
quòd Caesaris consilium hiemandi in Galliâ omnibus
cognitum est, frumentum his in locis in hiemem non
provisum erat.

20. Quibus rebus cognitis, principes Britanniae, qui
post proelium ad Caesarem convene- Overjoyed at Roman 185
rant, inter se colloquuntur. Romanis misfortunes the Britons renew hostili-
deesse equites et naves et frumentum ties.
intelligunt ; et paucitatem militum ex castrorum exi-

guitate cognoscunt : quae castra hoc erant etiam angus-
190 tiora, quod sine impedimentis Caesar legiones transportaverat. Constituunt, rebellione factâ, nostros frumento
commeatuque prohibere, et rem in hiemem producere;
his superatis aut reditu interclusis, neminem postea in
Britanniam transiturum belli inferendi causâ confidunt.
195 Itaque rursus conjuratione factâ, paulatim ex castris
discedere, ac suos clam ex agris deducere coeperunt.

21. Caesar nondum eorum consilia cognoverat :
Caesar repairs the tamen et ex eventu navium suarum et
shattered fleet. ex eo, quod obsides dare intermiserant,
200 fore id, quod accidit, suspicabatur.   Itaque ad omnes
casus subsidia comparabat.   Nam et frumentum ex agris
quotidie in castra conferebat, et materiâ atque aere earum navium, quae gravissime afflictae erant, ad reliquas
reficiendas utebatur; alia, quae ad eas res usui erant, ex
205 continenti comportari jubebat. Quae res summo studio
a militibus administrabatur: itaque, duodecim navibus
amissis, reliquis ut navigare commode posset, effecit.

22. Dum ea geruntur, una legio, quae appellabatur
The Romans sur- septima, ex consuetudine frumentatum
prised by an ambus-
210 cade of the Britons. missa est: nulla ad id tempus suspicio
belli interposita erat: pars hominum in agris remane-
bat, pars etiam in castra ventitabat : ii, qui pro portis
castrorum in statione erant, Caesari nuntiaverunt pul-
verem magnum atque inusitatum in eâ parte videri,
215 quam in partem legio iter fecisset.   Caesar aliquid novi
consilii a barbaris initum esse suspicabatur.   Itaque

cohortes, quae in stationibus erant, secum in eam
partem proficisci jussit : duas ex reliquis cohortes in
stationem succedere, reliquas armari et confestim sese
subsequi jussit. 23. Quum paulo longius a castris pro- 220
cessisset, suos ab hostibus premi animadvertit : con-
fertâ legione, ex omnibus partibus tela conjiciebantur.
Nam omni frumento ex reliquis partibus demesso, pars
una erat reliqua : hostes suspicati nostros huc esse
venturos noctu in silvis delituerant : tum subitò 225
nostros dispersos adoriuntur : nam illi, occupati in
metendo, arma deposuerant : itaque, paucis interfectis,
reliquos incertis ordinibus perturbant : simul equitatu
atque essedis nostros circumdant.

24. Genus hoc est ex essedis pugnae. Primo per 230
omnes partes perequitant, et tela conji- British mode of fight-
ciunt : ipso terrore equorum et strepitu chariots.
rotarum ordines plerumque perturbantur : tum quum se
inter turmas equitum insinuaverunt, ex essedis desili-
unt, et pedibus proeliantur. Aurigae interim paulatim 235
ex proelio excedunt : atque ita currus collocant ut,
si essedarii a multitudine hostium premantur, expedi-
tum ad suos receptum habeant. 25. Ita mobilitatem
equitum, stabilitatem peditum in proeliis praestant :
ac tantum usu et quotidianâ exercitatione efficiunt, ut 240
in declivi ac praecipiti loco incitatos equos sustinere
possint : et brevi spatio eos moderari ac flectere, et
per temonem percurrere, et in jugo insistere, et se
inde in currus citissime recipere solent.

Nostri milites novitate pugnae perturbantur: quibus

245 Caesar's arrival on the scene stops the battle. Taking advantage of the delay caused by storms, the Britons increase their forces for a fresh attack.

tempore opportunissimo Caesar auxilium tulit: namque ejus adventu hostes constiterunt, nostri se ex timore receperunt.   26. Sed Caesar alienum esse tempus ad committendum proe-

250 lium arbitrabatur: ita suo se loco continuit, et post aliquid temporis in castra legiones reduxit.   Dum haec geruntur, nostri omnes occupati sunt: reliqui, qui erant in agris, discesserunt.   Tempestates continuos complures dies secutae sunt: quae et nostros in castris

255 continebant, et hostem a pugnâ prohibebant.   Interim barbari nuntios in omnes partes dimiserunt, paucitatemque nostrorum militum suis praedicaverunt: et demonstraverunt, quanta daretur facultas praedae faciendae ac libertatis occupandae, si Romanos castris

260 expulissent.   Itaque, magnâ multitudine peditatûs equitatûsque coactâ, ad castra venerunt.

27. Caesar autem animadvertit hostes, si pellerentur,

The Roman camp attacked. The Britons routed and pursued with slaughter.

celeritate periculum effugere posse: quae res superioribus diebus acciderat.

265 Itaque nactus equites circiter triginta quos Commius Atrebas secum transportaverat, legiones in acie pro castris constituit.   Hostes, commisso proelio, diutius impetum nostrorum militum ferre non potuerunt, ac terga verterunt.   Quos nostri spatio

270 brevi secuti sunt: complures ex iis occiderunt; deinde, omnibus longe lateque aedificiis incensis, se in castra

receperunt. Eodem die legati ab hostibus missi ad
Caesarem de pace venerunt. **28.** His Caesar nume-
rum obsidum, quem antea imperaverat, The Britons surrender, and Caesar returns to Gaul.
duplicavit: eosque in continentem ad- returns to Gaul. 275
duci jussit. Ipse, idoneam tempestatem nactus, paulo
post mediam noctem naves solvit: quae omnes incolumes ad continentem pervenerunt: sed ex iis onerariae
duae portus capere non potuerunt, et paulo infra
delatae sunt. 280

Caesar in Belgis omnium legionum hiberna constituit.
Eò duae civitates ex Britanniâ obsides Preparations made during the winter for
miserunt, reliquae neglexerunt. Ro- a second invasion to
mae ex litteris Caesaris dierum viginti be undertaken in the following summer.
supplicatio a senatu decreta est. Interim naves aedifi- 285
cari veteresque refici jubet: ipse in fines Trevirorum
profectus est, quod hi neque ad concilia veniebant
neque imperio parebant. **29.** Inde ad portum Itium
pervenit, quò naves convenire jusserat, quòd inde erat
brevissimus in Britanniam trajectus. Dies circiter 290
viginti quinque in eo loco commoratus est, quòd
Corus ventus navigationem impediebat, qui mag-
nam partem omnis temporis his in locis flare consuevit. Tandem idoneam nactus tempestatem milites
equitesque conscendere in naves jubet. Labienum in 295
continente cum tribus legionibus et millibus duobus
equitum relinquit, ut portus tueatur et frumentum
provideat. Ipse cum quinque legionibus et pari
numero equitum, quem in continente reliquerat, ad

300 solis occasum naves solvit.   30. Primo leni Africo

The fleet crosses the provectus est : mox tamen mediâ cir-
Channel. Its appear-
ance strikes terror citer nocte, vento intermisso, cursum
into the Britons.
non tenuit et aestu longius delatus
est : ortâ luce sub sinistra Britanniam relictam con-
305 spexit.   Tum rursus aestus commutationem secutus
remis contendit, ut eam partem insulae caperet, quâ
optimus esset egressus.   Quâ in re militum virtus
admodum fuit laudanda ; qui vectoriis gravibusque
navigiis remigandi laborem non intermiserunt : itaque
310 longarum navium cursum adaequârunt. 31. Accessum
est ad Britanniam omnibus navibus meridiano fere
tempore, neque in eo loco hostis est visus : sed, ut
Caesar postea ex captivis cognovit, quum magnae
manus eò convenissent, multitudine navium perterriti
315 erant ; statim a litore discesserant ac se in superiora
loca abdiderant.   Caesar exercitum exposuit et
locum castris idoneum cepit : ex captivis cognovit,

Caesar lands his quo in loco hostium copiae conse-
troops. The enemy
are discovered in a dissent : cohortibus decem praesidio
forest inland. Caesar
320 dislodges them. navibus Q. Atrium praefecit. Ad
mare reliquit et equites trecentos, qui praesidio
navibus essent.   Ipse de tertiâ vigiliâ ad hostes
contendit.   Noctu progressus millia passuum circiter
duodecim, hostium copias conspicatus est. 32. Illi,
325 equitatu atque essedis ad flumen progressi, ex loco
superiore nostros prohibere et proelium committere
coeperunt. Repulsi ab equitatu se in silvas abdide-

Slinger. (Schreiber-Anderson.)

Sling-bolts. (Schreiber-Anderson.)

Testudo. (Schreiber-Anderson.)

runt, locum nacti egregic et natura et opere munitum :
nam, crebris arboribus succisis, omnes introitus erant
praeclusi.   Ipsi ex silvis rari propugnabant, nostrosque 330
intra munitiones ingredi prohibebant.   At milites
legionis septimae, testudine factâ, et aggere ad munitiones adjecto, locum ceperunt : eosque ex silvis
expulerunt, paucis vulneribus acceptis.   Sed eos fugi-
entes longius Caesar prosequi vetuit : nam loci naturam 335
ignorabat : magna pars diei jam consumpta erat ;
munitioni castrorum tempus relinqui volebat.

33. Postero die mane, tripartito milites equitesque in

Next day he is pre- expeditionem misit, ut eos, qui fuge-
vented from pursuit
by the news that the rant, persequerentur.   Hi aliquantum 340
fleet had been nearly
destroyed by a gale itineris progressi sunt, et jam paene
in the night.
erant in prospectu hostium ; sed
equites a Q. Atrio ad Caesarem venerunt, qui
nuntiarent superiore nocte, maxima coorta tempestate, prope omnes naves afflictas atque in litore 345
ejectas esse, quod neque ancorae funesque subsisterent,
neque nautae gubernatoresque vim tempestatis pati
possent : itaque ex eo concursu navium magnum
incommodum esse acceptum dixerunt.

34. His rebus cognitis, Caesar legiones equitatumque 350

Working night and revocari atque in itinere resistere
day for ten days, the
Romans repair their jubet, ipse ad naves revertitur : eadem
fleet, which is safely
beached.   fere, quae ex nuntiis litterisque
cognoverat, coram perspicit : naves circiter quadraginta erant amissae : reliquae tamen refici posse 355

magno negotio videbantur. Itaque ex legionibus
fabros deligit, et ex continenti alios arcessi
jubet: ipse, etsi res erat multae operae ac
laboris, tamen commodissimum esse statuit omnes
360 naves subduci, et cum castris unâ munitione conjungi:
in his rebus circiter dies decem consumit: ne noctu
quidem labor intermittitur: naves subducunt, et castra
egregie muniunt.   **35.** Tum Caesar easdem copias,

Caesar once more   quas ante, praesidio navibus reliquit,
365 makes for the in-   et eòdem, unde redierat, profectus
terior, where he
finds the Britons   est. Eò quum venisset, majores copiae
gathering under Cas-
sivellaunus.   Britannorum jam undique in eum

locum convenerant: summa imperii bellique administrandi communi consilio Cassivellauno permissa
370 erat: cujus fines a maritimis civitatibus flumen
dividit, quod appellatur Tamesis, a mari circiter
millia passuum octoginta. Huic superiore tempore
cum reliquis civitatibus continentia bella interces-
serant; sed nostro adventu permoti, Britanni hunc
375 toti bello imperioque praefecerant.

36. Insula naturâ est triquetra, cujus unum latus
Description of   est contra Galliam. Hujus lateris
Britain.   alter angulus, quò fere omnes ex Galliâ

naves appelluntur, ad orientem solem, inferior ad
380 meridiem spectat. Hoc pertinet circiter millia
Dimensions, &c.   passuum quingenta. Alterum vergit
ad Hispaniam atque occidentem solem: quâ ex parte
est Hibernia, dimidio minor, ut aestimatur, quam

Britannia, sed pari spatio transmissus atque ex
Gallia est in Britanniam. In hoc medio cursu est 385
insula, quae appellatur Mona : complures praeterea
insulae minores subjectae esse existimantur : de
quibus insulis nonnulli scripserunt dies continuos
triginta sub brumâ esse noctem. **37**. Nos nihil de eo
percontationibus reperiebamus, nisi certis ex aquâ 390
mensuris breviores esse quam in continenti noctes
videbamus. Hujus lateris est longitudo, ut fert
illorum opinio, septingentorum millium. Tertium
est contra septentriones : cui parti nulla est objecta
terra, sed ejus angulus lateris maxime ad Germaniam 395
spectat. Hoc millia passuum octingenta in longi-
tudinem esse existimatur. Ita omnis insula est in
circuitu vicies centum millium passuum.

Britanniae pars interior ab iis incolitur, quos natos
esse in insulâ ipsi dicunt : maritima *Its inhabitants, and* 400
pars ab iis, qui praedae ac belli *products.*
inferendi causâ ex Belgis transierunt : (qui omnes fere
iis nominibus civitatum appellantur, quibus orti ex
civitatibus cò pervenerunt): et, bello illato, ibi perman-
serunt, atque agros colere coeperunt. **38**. Hominum 405
est infinita multitudo, creberrimaque aedificia, fere
Gallicis consimilia ; pecorum magnus est numerus.
Utuntur aut aere aut taleis ferreis ad certum pondus
examinatis pro nummo. Nascitur ibi plumbum
album in mediterraneis regionibus : in maritimis 410
ferrum, sed ejus exigua est copia : aere utuntur

importato.   Materia cujusque generis ut in Galliâ
est praeter fagum atque abietem.   Leporem et galli-
nam et anserem gustare fas non putant : haec tamen
415 alunt animi voluptatisque causâ.   Loca sunt tempera-
tiora quam in Galliâ, remissioribus frigoribus.

39. Ex his gentibus longe sunt humanissimi, qui
Manners and cus-
toms of the Britons. Cantium incolunt: quae regio est maritima omnis, neque multum a Gallicâ
420 differunt consuetudine.   Interiores plerique frumenta
non serunt, sed lacte et carne vivunt, pellibusque sunt
vestiti.   Omnes vero se Britanni vitro inficiunt, quod
caeruleum efficit colorem, atque hoc horridiores sunt
in pugnâ aspectu ; capillum habent promissum ;
425 omnem corporis partem praeter caput et labrum
superius radunt.

Equites hostium essedariique acriter proelio cum
An indecisive en-
gagement with the
Britons. equitatu nostro in itinere conflix-
erunt : nostri tamen omnibus parti-
430 bus superiores fuerunt, atque eos in silvas collesque
compulerunt : sed, compluribus interfectis, cupidius
insecuti nonnullos ex suis amiserunt.   **40.** At illi,
intermisso spatio, subitò se ex silvis ejecerunt,
impetumque in eos fecerunt, qui erant in statione
435 pro castris collocati.   Nostri autem imprudentes
erant atque in munitione castrorum occupati : hostes
acriter pugnaverunt : et, nostris novo genere pugnae
perterritis, per medios audacissime perruperunt, seque
inde incolumes receperunt.   Eo die Q. Laberius

Durus, tribunus militum, interficitur.   Illi, pluribus 440
cohortibus submissis, repelluntur.

Postero die procul a castris suis hostes in collibus constiterunt: rari se ostenderunt : Followed next day
et lenius quam pridie nostros equites for the Romans.
by a great victory
proelio lacessere coeperunt.   41. Sed meridie quum 445
Caesar pabulandi causâ tres legiones atque omnem equitatum cum Gaio Trebonio legato misisset, repente ex
omnibus partibus ad pabulatores advolaverunt, sic uti
ab signis legionibusque non absisterent.   Nostri acriter
in eos impetu facto reppulerunt, neque finem sequendi 450
fecerunt, quoad subsidio confisi equites, quum post se
legiones viderent, praecipites hostes egerunt.   Magnus
numerus hostium interfectus est: nam nostri iis
neque sui colligendi neque consistendi aut ex essedis
desiliendi facultatem dederunt.   Ex hâc fugâ protinus 455
quae undique convenerant auxilia discesserunt ; neque
post id tempus unquam summis copiis nobiscum
hostes contenderunt.

42. Caesar, cognito consilio eorum, ad flumen Tame-
sim in fines Cassivellauni exercitum Caesar crosses the 460
duxit : quod flumen uno omnino loco Thames.
pedibus, atque hoc aegre, transiri potest.   Eò quum
venisset, vidit magnas hostium copias ad alteram flumi-
nis ripam esse instructas.   Ripa autem erat acutis sudi-
bus munita ; sudesque ejusdem generis sub aquâ defixae 465
flumine tegebantur.   Caesar, his rebus cognitis, equitatum praemittit : legiones confestim subsequi jubet.

Sed milites eâ celeritate atque eo impetu iêrunt, quum
capite solo ex aquâ exstarent, ut hostes impetum
470 legionum atque equitum sustinere non possent : ripas
dimiserunt ac se fugae mandaverunt.

43. Cassivellaunus omnem contentionis spem de-

Cassivellaunus, ponit : ampliores copias dimittit :
not wishing to risk
another battle, har- millibus circiter quattuor essedario-
asses the Roman
475 march by irregular rum relictis, itinera nostra servabat :
skirmishes and am-
buscades. paulum ex viâ excedebat : locis impe-
ditis ac silvestribus se occultabat : in iis regionibus,
quibus nos iter facturos esse cognoverat, pecora atque
homines ex agris in silvas compellebat : tum, quum
480 equitatus noster praedandi vastandique causâ se in
agros ejecerat, omnibus viis notis semitisque essedarios
ex silvis emittebat : ita magno cum periculo nostrorum
equitum cum iis confligebat, atque hoc metu latius
vagari prohibebat.   Itaque Caesar equites non longius
485 ab agmine legionum discedere passus est.

44. Interim Trinobantes, prope firmissima earum

The Trinobantes sub- regionum civitas, legatos ad Caesarem
mit to Caesar. Other
tribes follow. mittunt, pollicenturque sese ei dedi-
turos atque imperata facturos : ex quâ civitate
490 Mandubracius adolescens ad Caesarem in Galliam
venerat : cujus pater in eâ civitate regnum obtinuerat,
interfectusque erat a Cassivellauno : ipse fugâ mortem
vitaverat.   Illi petunt, ut Caesar Mandubracium ab
injuriâ Cassivellauni defendat, atque in civitatem
495 mittat.   His Caesar imperat obsides quadraginta,

frumentumque exercitui; Mandubraciumque ad eos
mittit. Illi imperata celeriter fecerunt : obsides ad
numerum frumentumque miserunt.

45. Ita Caesar Trinobantes defendit atque milites ab
omni injuria prohibuit : mox etiam Caesar's attack on 500
Cenimagni, Segontiaci, Ancalites, Verulamium (S. Al-bans), the strong-
Bibroci, Cassi, legationibus missis, hold of Cassivellau-nus.
sese Caesari dedunt. Ab his cognoscit non longe ex
eo loco oppidum Cassivellauni abesse, silvis paludi-
busque munitum, quò magnus hominum pecorisque 505
numerus convenerit. Oppidum autem Britanni vocant,
quum silvas impeditas vallo atque fossâ muniêrunt,
quò incursionis hostium vitandae causâ convenire
consuêrunt. Eò proficiscitur cum legionibus : locum
reperit egregie naturâ atque opere munitum : tamen 510
hunc duabus ex partibus oppugnare contendit. Hostes,
paulisper morati, militum nostrorum impetum non
tulerunt, seseque aliâ ex parte oppidi ejecerunt.
Magnus ibi numerus pecoris repertus est : multique
in fugâ sunt comprehensi atque interfecti. 515

46. Dum haec in his locis geruntur, Cassivellaunus ad
Cassivellaunus urges Cantium, quibus regionibus quattuor
the four chieftains of
Kent to attack the reges praeerant, Cingetorix, Carvilius,
camp on the shore.
Defeat of the Britons. Taximagulus, Segovax, nuntios mittit:
Cassivellaunus him-
self submits to his imperat, ut, coactis omnibus 520
Caesar. copiis, castra navalia de improviso
oppugnent. Ii quum ad castra venissent, nostri
eruptionem fecerunt : multos eorum interfecerunt :

Lugotorigem, ducem nobilem, ceperunt. Cassivellau-
525 nus, hoc proelio nuntiato, tot detrimentis acceptis,
vastatis finibus, maxime etiam defectione civium per-
motus est : legatos per Atrebatem Commium de dedi-
tione ad Caesarem mittit. Caesar, quum constituisset
hiemare in continenti propter repentinos Galliae motus,
530 neque multum aestatis superesset, obsides imperat :
constituit quid vectigalis in singulos annos populo
Romano Britannia penderet : imperat Cassivellauno,
ne Mandubracio neu Trinobantibus noceat.

47. Obsidibus acceptis, exercitum reducit ad mare,
535 Caesar returns to naves invenit refectas. His deductis,
Gaul to winter quar-
ters.   quòd et captivorum magnum numerum habebat, et nonnullae tempestate deperierant
naves, duobus commeatibus exercitum reportare
instituit. Ac sic accidit, ut ex tanto navium numero,
540 tot navigationibus, neque hoc neque superiore anno,
ulla omnino navis, quae milites portaret, desideraretur:
at ex iis, quae inanes ex continenti ad eum remitte-
bantur, militibus prioris commeatus expositis, per-
paucae locum ceperunt : reliquae fere omnes rejectae
545 sunt. Quas quum aliquamdiu Caesar frustra expecta-
visset, ne anni tempore a navigatione excluderetur,
quòd aequinoctium suberat, necessario angustius
milites collocavit : summa tranquillitas consecuta est :
initâ vigiliâ secundâ, naves solvit : primâ luce terram
550 attigit omnesque incolumes naves perduxit.

NOTES.

The Numbers refer to the lines of the Text.

3. Proficisci statuit. Caesar was at this time in N. Gaul: he had just been fighting the Suevi and other tribes near the Rhine.

6. loca. The usual plural form of **locus**: **loci** means *topics, places in books* generally.

13. ea, acc., object of reperire.

16. navi longa, a ship of war. Roman ships of war were long and narrow to ensure speed.

18. Morinos. See map. The most northerly people of Gaul. Virg. *Æn.* viii. 727, Extremique hominum Morini.

21. Veneticum bellum, the war with the Veneti. See map. They were a sea-faring tribe, and had possessed a large fleet, which Caesar had just destroyed in battle.

26. dare...obtemperare. Verbs like volo, possum, videor, etc., are incomplete in meaning without an infinitive, which is called *prolative*.

    imperio. Dative after obtempero = I am obedient *to.*

29. Commium. A Gaulish king, chief of the tribe of the Atrebates. They had been defeated by Caesar, and he had appointed Commius to be their king.

33. magna. Supply 'esse,' to be taken with **habebatur.**

37. quae viderit. Viderit is subjunctive because it is not stated as a *fact*, but as a *representation* of Volusenus.

40. Legati. Legatus will be found in Caesar with *two* meanings, to be decided by the context: (1) a *herald* or *ambassador;* (2) a *lieutenant-general*, or *adjutant* to the Imperator.

42. populo. Dative case of the remoter object.

45. propter anni tempus. The summer was growing late. It was now towards the end of August.

47. His. Dative of remoter object.

48. eos in fidem recipit = 'receives their submission.'

49. cogit = 'presses into his service.'

50. numero. Abl. of respect.

52. quaestores. The **quaestores** had charge of all money matters : they sometimes took command.

legatis. See above, l. 40 (2). Caesar had ten *legati* in Gaul. They were sometimes entrusted with separate commands.

praefectis. The **praefecti militum** commanded the auxiliary troops, or had special duties apart from the legion.

53. accedebant = came = 'were added.'

54. ab millibus passuum. Mille passus or **millia passuum** = 1000 paces, 1600 English yards. **Ab** here denotes not merely *distance* or *separation* from, but also the *measure* of the distance. Translate, 'at a distance of eight miles from,' etc.

61. tertia vigilia. The period between sunset and sunrise was divided into four equal parts called *vigilia*, distinguished as *prima, secunda. tertia, quarta vigilia*, each *vigilia* containing three *horae noctis*. Of course the length of the *vigiliae* varies, being longest in winter, and shortest in summer.

62. ulteriorem portum. If Caesar sailed from Itius, and if Itius is Wissant, this *ulterior portus* where the cavalry embarked should be Sangatte.

64. hora circiter quarta. The day would begin about 5 a.m., and this would therefore be about 9 o'clock. The Roman day from sunrise to sunset was divided into twelve equal parts, called *horae*, varying according to the season. **Circiter** is an adverb here.

69. angustis = 'precipitous.' **angustus** (from *ango*) = drawn in, contracted, hence 'having no slope.'

72. nequaquam idoneus, that is, for landing.

75. tribunos militum = military tribunes. There were six in each legion, but only one was on duty at a time. He had entire charge of the discipline when the soldiers were in camp.

77. **secundum. secundus** is really a participle from **sequor,** I follow : hence applied to wind and tide=favourable.

84. **essedarii. essedum,** from which **essedarii** comes, is a word of Gallic, not Latin, derivation : it was a two-wheeled chariot.

85. **hoc genere.** Abl. after **uti.** The verbs that take an abl. after them are **fungor, fruor, utor, vescor, dignor, potior,** and a few more : **uti** is prolative infinitive.

87. **reliquis copiis.** Abl. of *manner.* **subsecuti,** 'following closely.'

90. **in alto** = 'in deep water.' Caesar means that the ships drew so much water that they could not be beached.

95. **ex arido** = 'from the dry beach.'

97. **insuefactos** = 'trained to go into the water.'

99. **imperiti** = 'inexperienced in.' Takes a gen. case.

105. **inusitatior** = 'somewhat strange.' Literally, 'stranger' (than the appearance of trading ships).

106. **motus ad usum expeditior** = 'their facility for steering was readier.'

107. **magno usui nostris fuit.** ' **Sum** ' admits a *dative* case as the *completion* of the *predicate* and a second dative of the *recipient.* Translate, 'was a great advantage to our men.'

110. **paulum modo** ¬ 'for a short time only.' **pedem referre,** to retreat.

111. **militibus cunctantibus.** Ablative absolute. See Exercise xiii.

112. **decimae legionis.** The 10th legion, the 'Fighting Tenth,' contained the pick of Caesar's troops. Under Caesar a legion consisted of about 3000 men. Each legion contained 10 cohorts of 300 men ; each cohort 3 maniples of 100 men ; and each maniple 2 centuries of 50. The men in each cohort stood ten deep. Usually on the field of battle the legion was drawn up in three lines. The principal standard of the legion was

the eagle, which was carried by one of the bravest soldiers in the first cohort, under the charge of the centurion of the first century.

121. pugnatum est ab utrisque=utrique **pugnaverunt.** This impersonal use of pugnare is common.

123. ordines servare='to keep their ranks.'

124. signa. Besides the eagle, each division of the legion had its own standard, usually carried in front of the division.

alius alia ex navi='some from one ship and some from another.'

125. quibuscumque, etc.='whenever they had come up with a standard.'

129. ab latere aperto='in the undefended flank.'

131. scaphas longarum navium='the men-of-wars' cutters.' **Scapha** is a Greek word, meaning 'scooped out.'

Speculatoria navigia='reconnoitring vessels.'

132. laborantes='in distress.'

137. insulam capere='to reach the island.'

139. simul atque='as soon as.' See l. 384 for explanation of **atque.**

146. oratoris modo='after the fashion of a herald.'

149. ignosceretur. Verbs taking a dative in the active are used impersonally in the passive. Translate, 'that pardon might be granted to them.'

151. quod...intulissent. Intulissent is subjunctive, because it states, not a *fact*, but what Caesar *said* they had done.

164. propius occasum. The preposition **prope** takes an accusative case after it: so do **propior** and **proximus**, adjectives derived from **prope** and **propius,** adverb. **sui,** objective genitive, 'with great peril to themselves.'

166. adversa nocte='as the night was unfavourable to them.'

168. luna plena. This full moon has been fixed as having happened on the night of the 30th and 31st August, B.C. 55.

170. incognitum. Because there are no tides in the Mediterranean.

174. administrandi='managing the ships.'

186. **Romanis. Sum** with its compounds, except **possum**, takes a dative.

189. **hoc ... quod** = 'for this reason ... because.' **hoc** is ablative.

192. **frumento prohibere.** Verbs of *preventing* take an ablative : observe also **reditu interclusis.**

198. **ex eventu navium** = 'from what had happened to his ships.' Objective genitive.

199. **ex eo quod** = 'from the fact that.'

205. **ex continenti.** Understand **terra** : *continuous, unbroken* land as opposed to an island.

208. **Dum ea geruntur. Dum** (= while) always takes the present indicative.

209. **frumentatum.** The supine in **um** is used to express a *purpose* after verbs of motion.

214. **in ea parte...quam in partem** = 'in that direction towards which' : this superfluous addition of the noun in a relative sentence is not uncommon in Cæsar. Compare i. 16, **diem instare, quo die,** etc.

216. **aliquid novi consilii.** The genitive after **aliquid, multum, plus, nihil,** is commoner than those words in agreement with the succeeding noun.

228. **incertis ordinibus** = 'the ranks being broken.'

230. **ex essedis** has the force of an adjective agreeing with *pugnae.*

234. **turmas.** The cavalry attached to each legion numbered 300, divided into 10 squadrons (*turmæ*) of 30 each.

243. **temonem...jugum,** 'the chariot-pole,' 'the yoke to hold the horses' necks together.'

248. **receperunt se** = recovered themselves.

250. **post aliquid temporis.** See l. 216.

253. **reliqui** = the rest of the Britons.

254. **dies.** Acc. of *duration* of time.

258. **daretur.** Subjunctive in *indirect* question. See Exercise.

267. **pro castris** = as a defence to the camp

269. **spatio brevi** = at a short interval.

273. **His.** Dative with notion of disadvantage.

274. **quem imperaverat**=which he had imposed : **imperare** with dat. of *person* and acc. of *thing* is common in this sense.

279. **infra**=to the south.

284. **ex litteris**=' in accordance with Caesar's despatches.'

285. **supplicatio.** When a general at the head of his army won a victory, the senate decreed a public thanksgiving (*supplicatio*) to the gods for a number of days in proportion to the greatness of the victory.

286. **Trevirorum.** The Treviri, who have given their name to Trèves or Trier, occupied a part of the district of the Belgæ between the Moselle and the Rhine.

288. **ad portum Itium.** The chief place of the Morini in those days : most probably the place now called Wissant.

292. **Corus.** A wind from the W.N.W.

298. **pari...quem. Par** is more frequently followed by *ac* or *quam.* Here it seems to be used like **idem** which is followed by *qui.* Translate—' with an equal number of cavalry to that which he had left.'

300. **Africo.** A wind from the W.S.W.

301. **circiter** is an adverb here : **nocte,** abl. of time *when.*

307. **esset.** Subjunctive, because it states not an actual *fact,* but a *possibility.*

316. **exposuit**=disembarked.

318. **consedissent.** Subjunctive in *indirect* question.

219. **cohortibus.** Dat. after **praefecit. praesidio,** dative of *purpose.* **navibus,** dative of *recipient.*

322. **de tertia vigilia. de** seems to mean 'at the beginning of.'

325. **equitatu.** Ablative of manner. **ad flumen.** Possibly the Stour.

330. **rari**=' in scattered knots.'

332. **testudine facta.** In attacking a wall or rampart the Roman soldiers locked their shields together over their heads for a protection against missiles from above. This was called a **testudo** or ' tortoise.'

332. aggere adjecto. **agger** was a bank of earth carried up to the base of the ramparts.

338. mane. An old indeclinable noun, used in the nom., acc., and abl. cases.

344. nuntiarent. Subj. expressing purpose, **qui = ut ei.**

346. subsisterent = 'maintained their hold.'

351. resistere = 'to halt.'

353. eadem fere, etc. = 'personally sees that the facts were almost as he had ascertained,' etc.

358. multae operae. *Genitive* of quality describing **res**.

390. subduci = 'to be beached.'

369. Cassivellaunus ruled over the country N. of the Thames. He was the most powerful chieftain of these parts, and to him was entrusted the supreme command of the British forces.

371. Tamesis. The Thames. Caesar reckons its distance from the coast by the length of his march from the coast to where he crossed, *i.e.*, 80 miles.

383. dimidio. Ablative of *measure*.

384. transmissus. Nom. case. **pari...atque**, 'the passage is of *about the same* length *as* it is from Gaul, etc.' **par...ac** is like **idem** or **simul ac**. The explanation of **ac** here is simple : *e.g.*, take **simul ac venit, vicit =** 'as soon as he came he conquered.' The full form was **simul vicit ac simul venit =** 'he came *and* conquered at the same time.' The phrase was afterwards shortened to **simul ac venit, vicit.**

386. Mona. Tacitus speaks of Anglesey under this name : but from the position Caesar must be referring to the Isle of Man. The **insulae minores** are probably islands on the W. coast of Scotland.

389. bruma. Contracted from **brevima**, old form of superlative *brevissima : i.e.*, time when the day is shortest—winter.

390. ex aqua mensuris. The clepsydron, a contrivance by means of which time is measured by water dropping from one vessel into another. **392. ut opinio fert**, as their opinion is.

400. ipsi = 'the inhabitants themselves.'

402. Belgis. There was a tribe called Belgae in Britain occupying parts of Hampshire and Sussex.

403. iis...pervenerunt = 'are called by the names of those tribes from which they originated before they came there:' for **civitatum, quibus ex civitatibus** see above, l. 214.

408. taleis ferreis = 'bars of iron.'

409. plumbum album = 'tin'; but Caesar cannot be correct in saying that it is found in the midland districts, as the tin mines of Cornwall are older than any historical record. Iron was worked in Sussex (*maritimis regionibus*), as it was until long after Caesar's time. Bronze probably came from Gaul.

415. animi causâ = 'for the sake of amusement.'

422. vitro = 'woad,' a plant used for dyeing blue.

427. The preceding remarks about Britain have been a diversion: the account is now resumed from the point where it was dropped in c. 35.

441. submissis = 'sent to their relief.'

443. rari = 'in scattered parties.'

447. C. Trebonio. Tribunus plebis B.C. 55, now a *legatus* under Caesar, was afterwards one of his assassins.

454. sui colligendi = 'of rallying themselves.'

457. summis copiis = 'with all their forces together.'

459. consilio. This was to fall back on the river Thames.

461. uno loco...transiri potest. See Introduction, p. xvii.

465. defixae = fastened down under the water.

475. servabat = 'kept our route in sight.'

479. quum...ejecerat. *Quum* may take the pluperf. indicative when a demonstrative (as **tum** here) precedes, more accurately marking the time.

482. periculo nostrorum, etc. Obj. gen. after **periculo.**

483. hoc metu = by fear of this.

485. agmine. *agmen* is the line of march: *acies*, the line of battle.

486. Trinobantes. The people of Essex.

487. firmissima = most warlike. *Civitas* Caesar uses rather loosely for both Gallic and British tribes.

494. Cassivellauni. Subjective genitive, after **injuria.**

495. His...imperat. See above, l. 274.

498. ad numerum = 'to the required number.'

501. The **Cenimagni** probably came from Norfolk, Suffolk, and Cambridge : the **Segontiaci** from parts of Hampshire and Berks : the **Ancalites** from Wilts : the **Bibroci** from Berks : the **Cassi** from Herts. The position of some of these tribes is very doubtful, but Berks seems to preserve the name of the **Bibroci,** and Cassiobury that of the **Cassi.**

504. **oppidum** : afterwards occupied by the Romans, who built the town of Verulamium upon it, the site of the present St. Albans.

531. **quid vectigalis.** See l. 216.

533. **neu. ne** repeated becomes **neu,** not **neque.**

541. **quae milites portaret** = for carrying soldiers. This is the force of the subjunctive here, which indicates a purpose.

543. **prioris commeatus** = of the former voyage.

547. **aequinoctium.** Caesar left Britain before the last week of September.

559. **vigilia secunda.** See l. 61.

ABBREVIATIONS.

abl., ablative.
acc., accusative.
adj., adjective.
adv., adverb.
comm., common.
comp., comparative.
conj., conjunction.
dat., dative.
defect., defective.
demons., demonstrative.
distrib., distributive.
f., feminine.
frequent., frequentative.
gen., genitive.
gov., governing.
imper., imperative.
impers., impersonal.
incept., inceptive.
indecl., indeclinable.
indef., indefinite.
infin., infinitive.
irreg., irregular.
lit., literally.

m., masculine.
n., neuter.
nom., nominative.
num., numeral.
part., participle.
pass., passive.
perf., perfect.
pl., plural.
poss., possessive.
prep., preposition.
pres., present.
pron., pronoun.
pronom., pronominal.
reflex., reflexive.
rel., relative.
sing., singular.
subst., substantive.
superl., superlative.
v.a., verb active.
v. dep., verb deponent.
v.n., verb neuter.
voc., vocative.

VOCABULARY.

(LATIN-ENGLISH.)

ab *or* **a**, *prep. gov. abl.*, by, from, away.

ab·d-o, -ere, dĭd-i, ·dĭt-um, *v.a.* 3, I hide.

abi-es, -ĕtis, *f.*, a pine tree, fir.

ab·sist-o, -ere, ·stĭt-i, ·stĭt-um, *v.n.* 3, I stand apart from.

ab·sum, ·esse, ·fui, *v.n.*, I am away, I am distant.

ac (at·que), *conj.*, and.

ac·cēd-o, -ere, ·cess-i, ·cess-um, *v.n.* 3, I approach, I am added (ad ; cedo, I go).

accept-us, *from* accipio.

access-um est, *from* accedo, it was approached.

ac·cĭd-o, -ere, -i (no supine), *v.n.* 3, to fall out, to happen (ad, upon ; cado, I fall).

ac·cip-io, -ere, ·cēp-i, ·cept-um, *v.a.* 3, I receive (ad ; capio, I take).

aci-es, -ei, *f.*, order *or* line of battle.

acrĭter, *adv.*, sharply, vigorously.

acūt-us, -a, -um, *adj.*, sharp, pointed.

ad, *prep. gov. acc.*, to, at, towards, for.

ad·aeq-uo, *v.a.* 1, I bring to an equality, I keep pace with (ad, to ; aequo, I make equal).

ad·dūc-o, -ere, ·dux-i, ·duct-um, *v.a.* 3, I lead to, I bring to.

ad·eo, ·ire, ·iv-i, *or* i-i, ·ĭt-um, *v.n. irreg.*, I go to, I approach.

ad·ig-o, -ere, ·ēg-i, ·act-um, *v.a.* 3, I drive to, I hurl to (ad ; ago, I drive).

adĭt-us, -ūs, *m.*, a means of approach.

ad·jic-io, -ere, ·jec-i, ·ject-um, v.a. 3, I throw upon, I add.

ad·ministr-o, v.a. 1, I manage, I carry out.

admodum, adv., very, exceedingly.

adolesc-ens, -entis, comm. gen., a youth.

ad·or-ior, -iri, -tus sum, v. dep. 4, I attack.

advent-us, -ūs, m., arrival (advenio, I come to).

advers-us, -a, -um, opposite, unfavourable.

ad·vol-o, v.n. 1, I fly to, I hasten.

aedific-ium, -ii, n., a building.

aedific-o, v.a. 1, I build.

aegre, adv., with difficulty, scarcely.

aequinoct-ium, -ii, n., the equinox (aequus, equal; nox, night).

ae-s, -ris, n., bronze, copper.

aest-as, -atis, f., summer.

aēstim-o, v.a. 1, I estimate, I reckon.

aes-tus, -tūs, m., the tide.

af·flict-o, v.a. 1, I toss (ad, to; fligo, I dash).

afflict-us, from affligo.

af·flīg-o, -ere, ·flix-i, ·flict-um, v.a. 3, I shatter, I damage (ad, to; fligo, I dash).

Afrĭc-us, -i, m., the south-west wind.

ager, agr-i, m., a field, territory.

agg-er, -ĕris, m., a mound.

ag·grĕg-o, v.a. 1, I flock to, I attach myself to (ad; grex, a flock).

ag-men, -mĭnis, n., a march, a column (of soldiers).

ag-o, -ere, ēg-i, act-um, v.a. 3, I do, I drive.

alacrĭt-as, -ātis, f., alacrity, ardour.

alb-us, -a, -um, adj., white.

ali-ēnus, -ēna, -ēnum, adj., belonging to another, unfavourable.

aliquamdiu, adv., for a considerable time.

aliquant-um, -i, n., somewhat, some portion. aliquant-us, -a, -um, adj., some.

alĭ·quis, alĭ·quid (fem. sing. and neut. pl. not used), somebody, something.

al-ius, -ĭa, -ĭud, adj., another (gen., alīus; dat., alii). alii... alii, some...others.

al-o, -ere, -ui, -ĭtum and -tum, v. a. 3, I rear, I keep.

al-ter, -tera, -terum (*gen.*, al-tĕríus ; *dai.*, al-tĕri), *adj.*, the one (of two) ; **alter...alter**, the one...the other.

alt-ĭtūdo, -ĭtūdĭnis, *f.*, depth.

alt-um, -i, *n.*, the deep, the open sea (alt-us, high, deep).

amiss-us, *from* amitto.

a·mitt-o, *v.a.* 3, I lose (*see* mitto).

ampl-ior, -ius, *comp. adj.*, the greater (amplus).

Ancălīt-es, -um, *m. pl.*, the Ancalites.

ancŏr-a, -ae, *f.*, an anchor.

angŭl-us, -i, *m.*, an angle, a corner.

angust-ior, *comp. of* angustus.

angustius, *compar. adv.*, more closely.

angust-us, -a, -um, *adj.*, narrow, contracted, steep.

anim·advert-o, -ere, -i, ·advers um, *v.a.* 3, I observe, I understand (animum, the mind; adverto, I turn towards).

anim-us, -i, *m.*, mind, amusement.

ann-us, -i, *m.*, a year.

ans-er, -ĕris, *m.*, a goose.

ante, *adv.*, before, previously ; *prep. gov. acc.*, before.

antea, *adv.*, previously, once.

apert-us, -a, -um, *adj.*, un-covered, exposed (aperio, to uncover).

appell-o, *v.a.* 1, I call.

ap·pell-o, -ere, ·pul-i, ·puls-um, *v.a.* 3, I drive to, I bring to.

ap·propinqu-o, *v.n.* 1, I draw near to, I approach (with *dative*).

aqu-a, -ae, *f.*, water.

aquil-a, -ae, *f.*, an eagle.

aquĭlĭf-er, -eri, *m.*, a standard bearer (aquila, an eagle ; fero, I carry).

arhitr·or, *v. dep.* 1, I think, I consider.

arb-or, -ŏris, *f.*, a tree.

ar·cess-o, -ere, -īvi, ītum, *v.a.* 3, I call, I send for (ad, to ; cedo, I go, I cause to go).

arĭd-um, -i, *n.*, dry land (aridus, dry).

arm-a, -orum, *n. pl.*, arms, weapons.

armament-a, -orum, *n. pl.*, tackling.

arm-o, *v.a.* 1, I arm, I furnish with arms.

aspect-us, -ūs, *m.*, appearance.

at, *conj.*, but, yet.

at·ting-o, -ere, ·tĭg-i, ·tact-um, *v.a.* 3, I touch on, I reach (ad ; tango, I touch).

atque, *conj.*, as, with (*after words denoting similarity*), (*see* ac).

Atrĕb-as, -ătis, *m.*, one of the Atrebates.

auctor-ĭtas, -itatis, *f.*, influence, authority.

audacissime, *superl. adv.*, very boldly (audacter).

audacter, *adv.*, boldly (audax, bold).

aud-eo, -ere, **aus**-us sum, *v. semi-dep.* 2, I dare.

aurīg-a, -ae, *m.*, a driver, a charioteer.

aut, *conj.*, or. **aut...aut**, either ...or.

autem, *conj.*, but, moreover.

auxĭli-or, *v. dep.* 1, I help.

auxil-ium, -ii, *n.*, help, succour.

barbăr-us, -i, *m.*, a barbarian.

Belg-ae, -ārum, *m. pl.*, the Belgae, the Belgians.

bell-um, -i, *n.*, a war, warfare.

Bibroc-i, -orum, *m. pl.*, the Bibroci.

brev-ior, -ius, *comp. adj.*, shorter (brevis).

brev-is, -e, *adj.*, short, small (*comp.*, **brev-ior** ; *superl.*, **brev-issimus**).

Britann-ia, -iae, *f.*, Britain.

Britann-i, -orum, *m. pl.*, the Britons.

brum-a, -ae, *f.*, winter.

C = Cai-us, -i, *m.*, Gaius.

caerule-us, -a, -um, *adj.*, deep blue.

Caes-ar, -ăris, *m.*, Caesar.

Caius, -i, *m.*, Gaius.

Cant-ium, -ii, *n.*, Cantium, Kent.

cap-illus, -illi, *m.*, the hair (caput, the head).

cap-io, -ere, **cēp**-i, **capt**-um, *v.a.* 3, I take, I reach, I seize, I capture.

cap-tīvus, -tīvi, *m.*, a prisoner (capio, I take).

cap-ut, -ĭtis, *n.*, the head.

car-o, -nis, *f.*, flesh.

Carvil-ius, -ii, *m.*, Carvilius.

Cass-i, -orum, *m. pl.*, the Cassi.

Cassivellaun-us, -i, *m.*, Cassivellaunus.

cas-us, -ūs, *m.*, chance, accidents (cado, I fall).

castr-a, -ōrum, *n. pl.*, a camp.

caus-a, -ae, *f.*, a cause, a reason.

caus-â, *adverbial abl.* (with *gen.* or *gerund* in -di), for the purpose of.

celer-ĭtas, -ĭtātis, *f.*, swiftness, speed (celer, swift).

celĕrĭter, *adv.*, quickly.

Cenimagn-i, -orum, *m. pl.*, the Cenimagni.

centum, *num. adj. indecl.*, a hundred.

cep-it, *from* capio.

certe, *adv.*, surely.

cert-us, -a, -um, *adj.*, certain, sure.

Cingĕtŏr-ix, -ĭgis, *m.*, Cingetorix.

circiter, *adv.*, about, nearly.

circuit-us, ūs, *m.*, a circumference.

circum·d-o, -are, ·dĕd-i, ·dăt-um, *v.a.* 1, I surround.

circum·sist-o, -ere, ·stĕt-i (no supine), *v.a.* 3, I stand round, I surround.

citissĭme, *superl. adv.*, with the utmost rapidity (cito, rapidly).

civ-is, -is, *comm. gen.*, a citizen.

civ-ĭtas, -ĭtātis, *f.*, a state.

clam, *adv.*, secretly, by stealth.

class-is, -is, *f.*, a fleet.

co·act-a, *from* cogo.

coep-io, -isse, -i, -tum, *def.*, *v.a. and n.* 3, I begin.

cognĭt-us, *from* cognosco.

co·gnosc-o, -ere, ·gnōv-i, ·gnĭt-um, *v.a.* 3, I make inquiry about, I ascertain. In perf. tense, I know.

cognōv-erat, *from* cognosco.

cō·g-o, -ere, co·ēg-i, co·act-um, *v.a.* 3, I collect, I compel (cum, together : ago, I drive).

cohor-s, -tis, *f.*, a cohort.

col·lĭg-o, -ere, ·lēg-i, ·lect-um, *v.a.* 3, I gather together, I collect (con ; lego, I gather).

coll-is, -is, *m.*, a hill.

col·loc-o, *v.a.* 1, I put, I place (con ; loco, I place).

col·loqu-or, -i, ·loquut-us, sum, *v. dep.* 3, I talk with, I confer with (con ; loquor, I speak).

col-o, -ere, -ui, cult-um, *v.a.* 3, I cultivate, I till.

cŏl-or, -ōris, *m.*, colour.

commeā-tus, -tūs, *m.*, supplies, provisions, a voyage.

com·mend-o, *v.a.* 1, I commit, I entrust.

com·mitt-o, *v.a.* 3, I entrust (with *dative*), I engage in.

Comm-ius, -ii, *m.*, Commius.

commode, *adv.*, advantageously.

commodissĭm-us, -a, -um, *superl. adj.*, most convenient, very advantageous.

σ

com·mor-or, *v. dep.* 1, I delay, I stop.

commun-is, -e, *adj.*, common.

commuta-tio, -tiōnis, *f.*, a change, an alteration.

com·păr-o, *v.a.* 1, I prepare.

com·pell-o, -ere, ·pŭl-i, ·puls-um, *v.a.* 3, I drive together, I force.

com·plĕ-o, ·plēre, ·plēv-i, ·plēt-um, *v.a.* 2, I fill up.

com·plur-es, -a, *adj.*, very many, several.

com·port-o, *v.a.* 1, I carry together, I collect.

com·prehend-o, -ere, -i, ·prehens-um, *v.a.* 3, I seize.

comprehens-us, *from* comprehendo.

concil-ium, -ii, *n.*, a meeting, a council.

concurs-us, -ūs, *m.*, a running together, a collision (concurro).

con·fer-o, -re, ·tul-i, collat-um, *v.a. irreg.*, I bring together, I collect, I attribute to.

confert-us, -a, -um, *adj.*, crowded together, close packed.

confestim, *adv.*, immediately.

con·fīd-o, -ere, ·fīs-us sum, *v.a. semi-dep.* 3, I am persuaded,

I am confident, *v.n.*, I rely upon.

con·firm-o, *v.a.* 1, I strengthen, I establish.

confis-us, *perf. part. of* confido.

con·flīg-o, -ere, ·flīx-i, ·flict-um, *v.n.* 3, I come into conflict, I engage (con ; fligo, I dash).

con·jĭc-io, -ere, ·jēc-i, ·ject-um, *v.a.* 3, I throw, I hurl.

con·jung-o, -ere, ·junx-i, ·junct-um, *v.a.* 3, I join together, I unite.

con·jura-tio, -tiōnis, *f.*, a plot (con ; juro, I swear).

con·scend-o, -ere, -i, ·scens-um, *v.a.* 3, I embark, I go on board (con ; scando, I mount).

con·sĕqu-or, *v. dep.* 3, I follow after, I pursue (*see* sequor).

con·sīd-o, -ere, ·sēd-i, ·sess-um, *v.n.* 3, I take my station, I encamp.

consil-ium, -ii, *n.*, a plan, a purpose, intention, counsel.

con·simil-is, -e, *adj.*, quite like (with *dat.*).

con·sist-o, -ere, ·stit-i, stĭt-um, *v.n.* 3, I halt, I stop, I take my stand.

con·spĭc-io, -ere, ·spex-i, ·spect-um, *v.a.* 3, I see, I observe.

con·spĭc-or, v. dep. 1, I see, I descry.

constit-erunt, from consisto.

con·stitu-o, -ere, -i, ·stitŭt-um, v.a. 3, I put, I station, I appoint, I draw up, I determine.

consu-erunt, from consuesco.

consuē-sco, -scere, -vi, -tum, v.n. incep. 3, I accustom myself.

consue-tūdo, -tudĭnis, f., custom, habit.

consuev-it, from consuesco.

con·sum-o, -ere, ·sumps-i, ·sumpt-um, v.a. 3, I spend, I pass.

con·tend-o, -ere, -i, ·tent-um, v.n. and a. 3, I strive, I contend, I proceed eagerly, I hasten.

content-io, -iōnis, f., a contest.

con·test-or, v. dep. 1, I call to witness, I invoke.

continen-s, -tis, f., the connected land, the mainland (continēre, to be continuous).

continen-s, -tis, pres. part. of contineo, continuous, constant.

con·tin-eo, v.a. 2, I confine, I shut in, I restrain (con, teneo).

con·tin-uus, -ua, -uum, adj., in succession (con ; teneo, I hold).

contra, prep. gov. acc., against, opposite to.

con·věn-io, -ire, ·věn-i, ·vent-um, v.n. 4, I come together, I assemble.

con·vŏc-o, v.a. 1, I call together, I assemble.

co·or-ior, -iri, -tus sum, v. dep. 4, I arise.

coort-us, from coorior.

cop-ia, -iae, f., a supply, plenty, a quantity ; plural, forces, troops.

coram, adv., personally ; prep., in the presence of.

corp-us, -ŏris, n., a body.

Cor-us, -i, m., Corus, i.e., the north-west wind.

creb-er, -ra, -rum, adj., frequent, numerous, many.

creberrim-us, -a, -um, superl. adj., very frequent, very numerous (creber, frequent).

culp-a, -ae, f., a fault.

cum, prep. gov. abl., with.

cunct-or, v. dep. 1, I delay, I hesitate.

cupidius, compar. adv., more eagerly, too eagerly (cupide).

curr-us, -ūs, *m.*, a chariot (curro, I run).

cur-sus, -sūs, *m.*, a running, a course (curro, I run).

dare, *see* do.

daretur, *from* do.

dat-urus, *from* do.

de, *prep. gov. abl.*, from, out of, concerning, during.

de improviso, unexpectedly.

decem, *num. adj. indecl.*, ten.

de·cern-o, -ere, ·crēv-i, ·crēt-um, *v.a.* 3, I decree, I decide.

dĕc-īmus, -īma, -īmum, *num. adj.*, tenth.

declīv-is, -e, *adj.*, sloping.

dēdĕc-us, -ŏris, *n.*, a disgrace, a dishonour.

ded-ērunt, *from* do.

dēdit-io, -iōnis, *f.*, a surrender (dedo).

de.d·o, -ere, ·dĭd-i, ·dĭt-um, *v.a.* 3, I give up, I surrender.

de.duc-o (*see* subduco), *v.a.* 3, I lead off, I withdraw, I launch.

deduct-us, *from* deduco.

defect-io, -iōnis, *f.*, a revolt, a defection.

de·fend-o, -ere, -i, ·fens-um, *v.a.* 3, I protect.

de·fer-o, *v.a. irreg.*, I bring down, I carry down (*see* fero).

de·fīg-o, -ere, ·fix-i, ·fix-um, *v.a.* 3, I fix down, I drive down.

de·inde, *adv.*, afterwards, then.

de·jic-io, -ere, ·jēc-i, ·ject-um, *v.a.* 3, I throw down, I drive down (de, down).

de·lat-us, *from* defero.

dē·lĭg-o, *v.a.* 1, I bind down, I fasten.

de·lig-o, -ere, ·lēg-i, ·lect-um, *v.a.* 3, I choose out, I select.

de·litesc-o, -ere, ·lit-ui (no supine), *v.n.* 3, I conceal myself (de, away ; latesco, I hide myself).

de·met-o, -ere, ·mess-ui, ·mess-um, *v.a.* 3, I mow, I cut down.

de·monstr-o, *v.a.* 1, I show, I point out.

de·per-eo, -ire, ·iv-i or ·i-i (no supine), *v.n.*, I am entirely destroyed.

dē·pon-o, -ere, ·pos-ui, ·posĭt-um, *v.a.* 3, I lay down, I lay aside, I give up.

desidĕr-o, *v.a.* 1, I desire, I miss (a thing).

de·sil-io, -ire, -ui, ·sult-um, *v.n.* 4, I leap down.

dē·sum, ·esse, ·fu-i, *v.n. irreg.*, I fail, I am wanting.

detriment-um, -i, *n.*, loss, damage.

de-us, -i, *m.*, a god.

dic-o, -ere, **dix**-i, **dict**-um, *v.a.* 3, I say.

di-es, -ei, *m. and f.*, a day, a time.

dif.fer-o, -re, **dis·tul**-i, **dī·lat**-um, *v.n. irreg.*, I am different.

difficul-tas, -tātis, *f.*, difficulty.

dimidi-um, -i, *n.*, a half.

dī.mitt-o (*see* mitto), *v.a.* 3, I send about, I dismiss, I quit.

dis.cēd-o, ·cre, ·cess-i, ·cess-um, *v.n.* 3, I depart.

discess-erant, *from* discedo.

dis·perg-o, -ere, ·pers-i, ·pers-um, *v.a.* 3, I disperse (dis, in different directions ; spargo, I scatter).

dis·trĭbu-o, -ere, -i, ·trĭbūt-um, *v.a.* 3, I distribute, I assign (dis, among several ; tribuo, I give).

diūtĭus, *adv.*, longer (*compar. of* diu).

dīvĭd-o, -ere, **divīs**-i, **divīs**-um, *v.a.* 3, I divide.

dix-erunt, *from* dico.

d-o, -are, **dĕd**-i, **dăt**-um, *v.a.* 1, I give, I put.

dom-us, -i *and* -ūs, *f.*, a house, a home.

duc-o, -ere, **dux**-i, **duct**-um, *v.a.* 3, I lead.

dum, *conj.*, whilst, until.

du-o, -ae, -o, *num. adj. pl.*, two.

duŏ·decim, *num. adj. indecl.*, twelve.

duodeviginti, *adj.*, eighteen.

duplĭc-o, *v.a.* 1, I double.

Dur-us, -i, *m.*, Durus.

dux, duc-is, *comm. gen.*, a leader, a chief.

ө *or* **ex**, *prep. gov. abl.*, from, out of, away from, according to.

effect-urus, *from* efficio.

ef·fic-io, -ere, ·fēc-i, ·fect-um, *v.a.* 3, I make, I carry out, I bring to pass.

ef·fŭg-io, -ere, ·fŭg-i, ·fugĭt-um, *v.a. and n.* 3, I flee away, I escape.

ego, *pers. pron.*, I.

e·grĕd-ior, -i, ·gress-us sum, *v. dep.* 3, I disembark.

egrĕgie, *adv.*, excellently, exceedingly well, strongly.

e·gress-us, *from* egredior.

egress-us, -ūs, *m.*, a landing-place.

ejicere se (*see* ejicio), to throw themselves out, to rush forth.

e·jic-io (*see* adjicio), *v.a.* 3, I cast out, I drive ashore.

e·mitt-o (*see* mitto), *v.a.* 3, I send out.

enim, *conj.*, for.

eò, *adv.*, thither, there, for this reason.

eo, ire, iv-i *or* **i**-i, **ĭt**-um, *v.n. irreg.*, I go.

eōdem, *adv.*, to the same place.

ĕqu-es, **-ĭtis**, *m.*, a horseman; *pl.*, cavalry.

ĕquit-ātus, **-ātūs**, *m.*, cavalry.

equ-us, -i, *m.*, a horse.

erupt-io, **-iōnis**, *f.*, a sortie, a sally (erumpo, I break out).

esse. *See* sum.

essed-ārius, -ārii, *m.*, a chariot warrior, charioteer.

essĕd-um, -i, *n.*, a war chariot.

et, *conj.*, and; **et...et**, both... and.

ĕtĭam, *conj.*, also, even.

etsi, *conj.*, even if, although.

e·vĕn-io, -ire, **·vĕn**-i, **·vent**-um, *v.n.* 4, I happen.

event-us, **-ūs**, *m.*, occurrence (evenire, to happen).

examin-o, *v.a.* 1, I weigh.

ex·ced-o, -ere, **·cess**-i, **·cess**-um, *v.n.*, 3, I go out, I withdraw.

ex·clud-o, -ere, **·clus**-i, **·clus**-um, *v.a.* 3, I prevent, I hinder (ex; claudo, I shut).

ex·cus-o, *v.a.* 1, I excuse.

exercitat-io, **-iōnis**, *f.*, exercise, practice.

exerc-ītus, -ītūs, *m.*, an army (exerceo, I exercise).

exigu-ĭtas, -ĭtātis, *f.*, small size (exiguus, small).

exigu-us, -a, -um, *adj.*, small, little.

ex·istim-o, *v.a.* 1, I think, I suppose (ex; aestimo).

expedī-tio, -tiōnis, *f.*, an expedition.

ex·pedīt-us, -a, -um, *part.*, unimpeded, ready, easy (*comp.*, expeditior).

ex·pell-o, -ere, **·pul**-i, **·puls**-um, *v.a.* 3, I drive out, I expel.

ex·pon-o, -ere, **·posu**-i, **·posĭt**-um, *v.a.* 3, I post, I draw up (ex, out, forth; pono, I place).

exposit-us, *from* expono, here = landed.

expos-uit, *from* expono.

ex·pul-erunt, *from* expello.

exspect-o, *v.a.* 1, I wait, I await.

ex·st-o, -are (*no perf. or supine*), *v.n.* 1, I stand out of.

fa-ber, -bri, *m.*, an artificer.

faci-endae, *from* facio.

făc-io, -ere, fēc-i, fact-um, *v.a.* 3, I make.

fact-us, *from* facio.

facul-tas, -tātis, *f.*, power, opportunity.

fag-us, -i, *f.*, a beech tree, beech.

fas, *n. indecl.*, the will of the gods, a lawful thing.

felĭcĭter, *adv.*, prosperously.

fēre, *adv.*, nearly, almost, about.

fer-o, -re, tul-i, lāt-um, *v.a. irreg.*, I bear, I carry.

ferre. *See* fero.

ĭerr-eus, -ea, -eum, *adj.*, made of iron, iron-.

ferr-um, -i, *n.*, iron.

fert, *from* fero.

fid-ēlis, ēle, *adj.*, faithful.

fĭd-es, -ei, *f.*, faith, engagement, protection.

figūr-a, -ae, *f.*, a form, a shape, appearance.

fin-is, is, *m.*, an end, a boundary ; *pl.*, borders, territory.

firm-issimus, -issima, -issimum, *superl. adj.*, strongest, most powerful (firmus).

firmĭter, *adv.*, firmly.

flect-o, -ere, flex-i, flex-um, *v.a.* 3, I turn.

fl-o, *v.n.* 1, I blow.

fluctus, -ūs, *m.*, a wave.

flu-men, -mĭnis, *n.*, a river (fluo, I flow).

fore, *from* sum.

fortun-a, -ae, *f.*, chance, fortune.

foss-a, -ae, *f.*, a ditch, a trench.

frang-o, -ere, frēg-i, fract-um, *v.a.* 3, I break, I wreck.

frig-us, -ŏris, *n.*, cold, coldness.

frument-or, *v. dep.* 1, I get corn, I forage.

frument-um, -i, *n.*, corn.

frustra, *adv.*, in vain.

fug-a, -ae, *f.*, flight.

fŭg-io, -ere, fūg-i, fŭgĭt-um, *v.n. and a.* 3, I flee.

fund-a, -ae, *f.*, a sling.

fun-is, -is, *m.*, a rope, a cable.

Gall-i, -orum, *m. pl.*, the Gauls.

Gall-ia, -iae, *f.*, Gaul.

Gallĭc-us, -a, -um, *adj.*, Gallic.

gallīn-a, -ae, *f.*, a hen.

gen-s, -tis, *f.*, a race, a nation, a people.

gen-us, -ĕris, *n.*, a race, a kind.

German-ia, -iae, *f.*, Germany.

gĕr-o, -ere, gess-i, gest-um, *v.a.* 3, I carry on, I do, I wage.

grav-is, -e, *adj.*, heavy.

gravissime, *adv.*, very seriously (*superl. of* graviter).

gubernā-tor, -tōris, *m.*, a pilot.

gust-o, *v.a.* 1, I taste.

hab-eo, *v.a.* 2, I have, I hold, I consider.

hibern-a, ōrum, *n. pl.*, winter quarters.

Hibern-ia, -iae, *f.*, Ireland.

hic, haec; hoc, *demons. pron.*, this.

hiem-o, *v.n.* 1, I winter, I take up winter quarters (hiems, winter).

hiem-s, -is, *f.*, winter.

Hispan-ia, -iae, *f.*, Spain.

hoc, *adverbial abl.*, on this account.

hom-o, -ĭnis, *comm. gen.*, a man, a person.

hōr-a, -ae, *f.*, an hour.

horrid-ior, -ius, *compar. adj.*, more terrible, more horrible (horridus).

hort-or, *v. dep.* 1, I exhort, I encourage.

hos-tis, -tis, *comm. gen.*, an enemy.

húc, *adv.*, hither.

human-issimus, -issima, -issimum, *superl. adj.*, most civilized (humanus).

ibi, *adv.*, there.

ĭ·dem, eă·dem, ĭ·dem, *demons. pron.*, the same.

ĭdōne-us, -a, -um, *adj.*, suitable, convenient.

ignōr-o, *v.a.* 1, I am unacquainted with.

i·gnosc-o, -ere, ·gnov-i, ·gnotum, *v.a. and n.* 3, I pardon, I overlook (*with dat.*), (in, not ; nosco, I know).

i·gnōt-us, -a, -um, *adj.*, not known, unknown (nosco).

illat-um, *from* infero.

ill-e, -a, -ud, *pron. demons.*, he, she, it, that.

illò, *adv.*, to that place, thither.

impĕdi-mentum, -menti, *n.* (*pl.*), baggage.

im·ped-io, *v.a.* 4, I impede, I hinder (in ; pes, a foot).

impedīt-us, *past part.*, impedio, obstructed.

imperā-tor, -tōris, *m.*, a commander, a general.

imperat-um, -i, *n.*, a command.

im·perīt-us, -a, -um, *adj.*, unskilful, not acquainted with (with *gen.*).

impĕr-ium, ii, *n.*, dominion, empire, a command.

imper-o, *v.a.* 1, I command, I order.

impĕt-us, -ūs, *m.*, an attack, an onset.

im·port-o, *v.a.* 1, I carry into, I import.

im·prōvīs-us, -a, -um, *adj.*, unexpected (in, not ; provideo, I foresee). **de improviso**, unexpectedly.

im·prud-ens, -entis, *adj.*, heedless, unwary (in, not ; prudens, foreseeing).

imprudent-ia, -iae, *f.*, imprudence, indiscretion.

in, *prep. with acc.*, into, for, against ; *with abl.*, in, on, at, upon.

inān-is, -e, *adj.*, empty.

in·cend-o, -ere, -i, ·cens-um, *v.a.* 3, I set on fire, I burn.

in·cert-us, -a, -um, *adj.*, uncertain.

incitat-us, -a, -um, *past part.*, at full speed, swift (incito).

in·cit-o, *v.a.* 1, I set in rapid motion, I urge forward.

in·cognit-us, -a, -um, *adj.* unknown (in, not ; cognitus, known).

incŏl-a, -ae, *comm. gen.*, an inhabitant.

in·col-o, -ere, -ui (*no supine*), *v.n. and a.* 3, I dwell, I inhabit.

in·colŭm-is, -e, *adj.*, quite safe, in safety.

incommod-um, -i, *n.*, trouble, disaster.

incur·sio, -siōnis, *f.*, an inroad, a raid (in ; curro, I run).

inde, *adv.*, from that place, thence.

in·eo, ·ire, ·iv-i *or* ·ĭt-um, *v.a. irreg.*, I form, I adopt, I begin.

infer·ior, -ius, *comp. adj.*, lower.

in·fer-o, -re, ·tul-i, il·lat-um, *v.a.*, I bring into, I make (war).

in·fic-io, -ere, ·fēc-i, ·fect-um, *v.a.* 3, I dip in, I dye.

infinīt-us, -a, -um, *adj.*, countless, infinite.

infra, *adv.*, below.

in·grĕd-ior, -i, ·gress-us, sum; *v. dep.* 3, I enter.

inĭt-us, *from* ineo.

injuri-a, -ae, *f.*, injustice, a wrong.

inquam, *v. def.*, I say.

in·sequ-or, *v. dep.* 3, I follow after.

in·sinu-o, *v.a.* 1, I make a way into (in ; sinuo, I wind).

in·sist-o, -ere, ·stĭt-i (no supine), *v.n.* 3, I stand.

in·stĭtŭ-o, -ere, -i, ·stĭtūt-um, *v.a.* 3, I resolve, I begin.

in·stru-o, -ere, ·strux-i, ·struct-um, *v.a.* 3, I build, I draw up (troops).

in·suē·fact-us, -a, -um, *adj.*, accustomed, *see note* (suesco, I accustom ; facio, I make).

insŭl-a, -ae, *f.*, an island.

intellĭg-o, -ere, ·lex-i, ·lect-um, *v.a.* 3, I perceive, I understand.

inter, *prep. gov. acc.*, between, among.

inter·cēd-o, -ere, ·cess-i, ·cess-um, *v.n.* 3, I intervene, I am between.

inter·clud-o, -ere, ·clus-i, ·clus-um, *v.a.* 3, I close up, I cut off (inter, between ; claudo, I shut).

interĕa, *adv.*, meanwhile.

interfect-us, *from* interficio.

inter·fic-io, -ere, ·fēc-i. ·fect-um, *v.a.* 3, I kill.

intĕrim, *adv.*, in the meantime.

inter·ior, -ius, *comp. adj.*, inner, interior.

intermiss-us, *from* intermitto, being allowed to intervene.

inter·mitt-o (*see* mitto), *v.a.* 3, I leave off, I relax.

inter·pon-o, -ere, ·posui, ·pos-

ĭtum, *v.a.* 3, I interpose. *Pass.*, I arise (inter ; pono, I place).

intra, *prep. gov. acc.*, within.

introĭt-us, -ūs, *m.*, an entrance, an approach.

in·usitāt-us, -a, -um, *adj.*, unusual, extraordinary (*comp.*, inusitatior).

in·util-is, -e, *adj.*, useless.

in·vĕn-io (*see* venio), *v.a.* 4, I find, I discover.

ips-e, -a, -um, *pron.*, self, very ; *as subst.*, himself.

is, ea, id, *pron.*, he, she, it, that.

ita, *adv.*, thus, so.

ita·que, *conj.*, and so, therefore.

item, *adv.*, so, also, in like manner.

i·teṛ, -tĭnĕris, *n.*, a march, a journey.

It-ius, -ii, *m.*, Itius.

jac-io, -ere, jēc-i, jact-um, *v.a.* 3, I throw.

jam, *adv.*, already, now.

jub-eo, -ere, juss-i, juss-um, *v.a.* 2, I order, I command.

jug-um, -i, *n.*, the yoke.

Laber-ius, -ii, *m.*, Laberius.

Labiēn-us, -i, *m.*, Labienus.

lab-or, -ōris, *m.*, toil, labour.

labor-o, *v.n.* 1, I labour, I am hard pressed.

labr-um, -i, *n.*, a lip.

lac, **lact**-is, *n.*, milk.

lacess-o, -ere, ·**īv**-i *or* ·i-i, ·**īt**-um, *v.a.* 3, I provoke, I attack.

late, *adv.*, widely.

lat-ius, *comp. adv.*, more widely.

lat-us, -ĕris, *n.*, a side, a flank.

laud-o, *v.a.* 1, I praise.

legat-io, -ionis, *f.*, an embassy.

legāt-us, -i, *m.*, an ambassador, a lieutenant.

leg-io, -iōnis, *f.*, a legion.

lēn-is, -e, *adj.*, gentle.

lenius, *comp. adv.*, more slowly, with less spirit (leniter, slowly).

lĕp-us, -ŏris, *m.*, a hare.

liberaliter, *adv.*, courteously, liberally.

liber-tas, -tātis, *f.*, liberty, freedom.

litter-a, -ae, *f. sing.*, a letter (of the alphabet) ; *pl.*, a letter, an epistle.

lĭt-us, -ŏris, *n.*, the sea-shore.

lŏc-us, -i, *m.* (*pl.* loc-i *and* loc-a), a place, a position.

longe, *adv.*, far off. **late**, *adv.*, widely. **longe lateque**, far and wide.

longinqu-us, -a, -um, *adj.*, far off, distant (*compar.*, longinquior).

longitūd-o, -ĭnis, *f.*, length.

longius, *adv.*, longer, farther.

long-us, -a, -um, *adj.*, long.

Lugotŏr-ix, -ĭgis, *m.*, Lugotorix.

lun-a, -ae, *f.*, the moon.

lux, **luc**-is, *f.*, light, daylight.

magn-itudo, -itudĭnis, *f.*, greatness, magnitude.

magn·ŏpĕre, *adv.*, greatly, exceedingly.

magn-us, -a, -um, *adj.*, great, large.

maj-or, us, *comp. adj.*, greater.

mandāt-um, -i, *n.*, a command, an order.

mand-o, *v.a.* 1, I command, I commit.

Mandubra-cius, -ii, *m.*, Mandubracius.

mane, *adv.*, early in the morning.

man-us, -ūs, *f.*, a hand, a band (of men).

mar-e, -is, *n.*, the sea.

mar-itĭmus, -itĭma, -itĭmum, *adj.*, of the sea, sea- ; on the sea-coast.

matĕr-ia, -iae, *f.*, wood, timber.

maxime, *superl. adv.*, in the

highest degree, chiefly, very greatly.

maxĭm-us, -a, -um, *superl. adj.*, greatest, very great (magnus, great).

medi·terr-aneus, -anea, -aneum, *adj.*, inland.

med-ius, -ia, -ium, *adj.*, middle. **media nox**, midnight.

mensur-a, -ae, *f.*, a measuring, measurement.

mercāt-or, -ōris, *m.*, a trader.

merīdi-ānus, -āna, -ānum, *adj.*, of mid-day. **meridianum tempus**, mid-day.

meri·di-es, -ei, *m.*, mid-day, the south.

mĕt-o (*see above*, de·meto), *v.a.* 3, I mow, I reap.

metŭ-o, -ere. -i (no sup.), *v.a. and n.* 3, I fear.

met-us, -ūs, *m.*, fear, dread.

me-us, -a, -um, *poss. pron.*, my, mine.

mĭl-es, -ĭtis, *comm. gen.*, a soldier.

milit-ia, -iae, *f.*, warfare.

milli-a, -um, *n. pl.*, a thousand.

min-or, -us, *compar. adj.*, less (*comp. of* parvus).

mis-erunt, *from* mitto.

miss-us, *from* mitto.

mitt-o, *v.a.* 3, I send.

mobĭl-itas, -itatis, *f.*, quickness, rapidity (mobilis, easily moved).

modĕr-or, *v. dep.* 1, I manage, I control, I check.

modo, *adv.*, only, merely.

mod-us, -i, *m.*, a manner, a way.

Mon-a, -ae, *f.*, Mona.

mon-s, -tis, *m.*, a mountain.

morat-us, *from* moror.

Morĭn-i, -orum, *m. pl.*, the Morini.

mor-or, *v.a. dep.* 1, I delay, I linger, I tarry.

mor-s, -tis, *f.*, death.

mot-us, -ūs, *m.*, a motion, a movement.

mox, *adv.*, soon, afterwards.

mult-ĭtūdo, -ĭtūdĭnis, *f.*, a multitude, the mass of the people.

multum, *adv.*, much, greatly.

mul-tus, -ta, -tum, *adj.*, much.

mun-io, *v.a.* 4, I fortify, I protect.

muni-tio, tiōnis, *f.*, a fortifying, a fortification (munio).

nact-us, *from* nanciscor.

nam, *conj.*, for.

namque, *conj.*, for indeed.

nancisc-or, -i, **nact**-us sum, *v. dep.* 3, I get, I obtain.

nasc-or, -i, nat-us sum, *v. dep.* 3, I am born, I am produced.

natur-a, -ae, *f.,* the nature.

nav-ālis, -āle, *adj.,* naval, sea-.

naviga-tio, -tiōnis, *f.,* a sailing.

nav·ig-o, *v.n.* 1, I sail (navis, a ship).

navĭg-ium, *n.,* a vessel.

nav-is, -is, *f.,* a ship.

naut-a, -ae, *m.,* a sailor.

ne, *adv.,* lest, that not.

ne quidem, not even.

necessārio, *adv.,* necessarily.

neglĭg-o, -ere, neglex-i, neglect-um, *v.a.* 3, I overlook, I neglect.

neg·ot-ium, -ii, *n.,* an affair, trouble (nec; otium, leisure).

nem-o, nullius, *n.,* nobody.

ne·quāquam, *adv.,* by no means.

nĕque, *conj.,* and not, nor; **neque...neque,** neither...nor.

neu, *conj.,* and not, nor.

nihil, *n. indecl.,* nothing.

nĭsĭ, *conj.,* if not, unless, except.

no-bilis, -bile, *adj.,* noble.

nobiscum = cum nobis.

noc-eo, *v.n.* 2, I hurt.

noct-es, *from* nox.

noctu, *adv. abl.,* by night.

nom-en, -ĭnis, *n.,* a name.

non, *adv.,* not.

nondum, *adv.,* not yet.

non·null-us, -a, -um, *adj.,* some.

non-us, -a, -um, *adj.,* ninth.

nos *pl. of* ego.

nosc-o, -ere, nōv-i, not-um, *v.a.* 3, I know.

nos-ter, -tra, -trum, *adj. pron.,* our; *as subst. pl. m.,* our men.

not-us, *perf. part.* from nosco.

nov-ĭtas, -ĭtātis, *f.,* newness, strangeness (novus, new).

nov-us, -a, -um, *adj.,* new.

nox, noct-is, *f.,* night.

n·ullus, ·ulla, ·ullum, *adj.,* not any, none, no (ne, not; ullus).

numĕr-us, -i, *m.,* a number.

numm-us, -i, *m.,* money.

nunti-o, *v.a.* 1, I announce.

nunt-ius, -ii, *m.,* a messenger.

ob, *prep. gov. acc.,* for, on account of.

ob·jic-io, -ere, ·jēc-i, ·ject-um, *v.a.* 3, I present (to view), I oppose (ob, before; jacio, I throw).

obs-es, -ĭdis, *comm. gend.,* a hostage.

ob·tempĕr-o, *v.n.* 1, I submit to, I obey (with *dative*).

ob·tin-eo, -ere, -ui, ·tent-um, *v.a.* 2, I hold, I acquire.

occās-us, -ūs, *m.*, the setting *or* going down (ob ; cado, I fall).

oc·cīd-o, -ere, -i, ·cīs-um, *v.a.* 3, I cut down, I kill (ob, against ; caedo, I strike).

oc·cīd-o, -ere, -i, ·cās-um, *v.n.* 3, I go down, I set.

occult-o, *v.a.* 1, I hide.

{ oc·cup-o, *v.a.* 1, I seize, I gain.
oc·cupat-us, *perf. part.*, engaged in.

oc·curr-o, -ere, -i, ·curs-um, *v.n.* 3, I run up to, I fall in with, I meet (ob, towards ; curro, I run).

ocĕăn-us, -i, *m.*, the ocean.

octingent-i, -ae, -a, *adj.*, eight hundred.

octo, *num. adj. indecl.*, eight.

octoginta, *num. adj.*, eighty.

offic-ium, -ii, *n.*, a duty, an office.

olim, *adv.*, at some time, formerly.

omn-ia, all things.

omnīno, *adv.*, altogether, wholly, in all.

omn-is, -e, *adj.*, all, every.

oner-arius, -aria, -arium, *adj.*, of *or* belonging to a burden (*see* note).

ŏn-us, -ĕris, *n.*, a burden, a load, a weight.

oper-a, -ae, *f.*, work, labour, aid

opin-io, -iōnis, *f.*, opinion.

oppid-um, -i, *n.*, a town, a city

opportun-issimus, -issima, -issimum, *superl. adj.*, most convenient, most opportune,

op·port-ūnus, -ūna, -ūnum, *adj.*, convenient, suitable, opportune.

op·prĭm-o, -ere, ·press-i, ·press-um, *v.a.* 3, I overwhelm, I overload (ob, against; premo, I press).

oppugn-o, *v.a.* 1, I attack, I besiege.

optim-us, -a, ·um, *superl. adj.*, best.

op-us, -ĕris, *n.*, work, a fortification.

or-a, *f.*, the coast.

orā-tor, -tōris, *m.*, an ambassador.

ord-o, -ĭnis, *m.*, order, a line, a rank.

ori-ens, *pres. part. from* orior.

or-ior, -iri, -tus sum, *v. dep.* 3 *and* 4, I rise, I spring from.

ort-i, *from* orior.

ostend-o, -ere, -i, osten-sum *and* -tum, *v.a.* 3, I show.

pabulat-or, -ōris, *m.*, a forager.

pabul-or, *v. dep.* 1, I forage.

paene, *adv.*, nearly, almost.

pal-us, -ūdis, *f.*, a swamp, a marsh.

par, par-is, *adj.*, equal.

par-eo, *v.n.* 2, I obey (with *dat.*).

par-i, *from* par.

par-o, *v.a.* 1, I prepare, I procure.

par-s, -tis, *f.*, a part, a side.

pass-us, -ūs, *m.*, a step, a pace.

pass-us sum, *from* patior.

pat-ior, -i, **pass**-us sum, *v. dep.* 3, I bear, I endure, I suffer.

pauc-ĭtas, -ĭtātis, *f.*, a small number.

pauc-us, -a, -um, *adj.*, small; *pl.*, few.

paulatim, *adv.*, by little and little, gradually.

paulisper, *adv.*, for a short time.

paulo, *adv.*, a little, somewhat.

paulum, *adv.*, a little, somewhat.

pax, pac-is, *f.*, peace.

pecor-a, *from* pecus.

pec-us, ŏris, *n.*, cattle.

ped-es, -itis, *m.* 3, a foot soldier; *pl.*, infantry.

peditāt-us, ūs, *m.*, foot soldiers, infantry.

pell-is, -is, *f.*, a skin.

pell-o, -ere, **pepŭl**-i, **puls**-um, *v.a.* 3, I rout, I put to flight.

pend-o, -ere, **pepend**-i *and* **pend**-i, **pens**-um, *v.a.* 3, I pay.

per, *prep. gov. acc.*, through, by, along.

percontat-io, -iōnis, *f.*, an enquiry.

per·curr-o, -ere, ·cucurr-i *or* ·curr-i, ·curs-um, *v.n.* 3, I run along.

per·duc-o, -ere, ·dux-i, ·duct-um, *v.a.* 3, I bring, I conduct.

per·ĕquĭt-o, *v.n.* 1, I ride through *or* hither and thither.

per·fĕr-o, -re, ·tul-i, ·lat-um, *v.a. irreg.*, I bear, I carry.

perīcŭl-um, -i, *n.*, an attempt, danger.

per·man-eo, -ere, -si, -sum, *v.n.* 2, I remain.

per·mitt-o (*see* mitto), *v.a.* 3, I give up, I entrust, I allow.

per·mŏveo, *v.a.* 2, I move deeply, I stir (*see* summoveo).

per·pauc-us, -a, -um, *adj.*, very little; *pl.*, very few.

per·rump-o, -ere, ·rūp-i, ·rupt-um, *v.n.* 3, I break through.

per·sequ-or, -i, ·secut-us sum, *v. dep.* 3, I pursue.

per·spic-io, -ere, ·spex-i, ·spect-um, *v.a.* 3, I perceive, I ascertain.

per·terr-eo, *v.a.* 2, I frighten thoroughly, I terrify greatly.

per·tin-eo, -ere, -ui, ·tent-um, *v.n.* 2, I reach, I extend.

perturba-tio, -tiōnis, *f.*, confusion.

per·turb-o, *v.a.* 1, I disturb utterly, I throw into confusion.

per·věn-io (*see* venio), *v.n.* 4, I come up, I arrive.

pes, pěd-is, *m.*, a foot.

pět-o, -ere, -īvi *and* -ii, ītum, *v.a.* 3, I seek, I beg.

plan-us, -a, -um, *adj.*, level, flat.

plē-nus, -na, -num, *adj.*, full (pleo, I fill).

plerumque, *adv.*, for the most part, generally.

plerusque, pleraque, plerumque, *adj.*, the greater part ; *pl.*, very many.

plumb-um, -i, *n.*, lead.

plumbum album = tin.

plures. *See* plus.

plus, plur-is, *comp. adj.*, more ; *pl.*, several, very many.

pol·lic-eor, -eri, -ītus sum, *v. dep. a. and n.* 2, I promise.

pond-us, -ěris, *n.*, a weight.

popul-us, -i, *m.*, the people.

port-a, -ae, *f.*, a gate.

port-o, *v.a.* 1, I carry.

port-us, -ūs, *m.*, a harbour.

pos·sum, po·sse, pot-ui, *v. irreg.*, I am able, I can (potis, able, *and* sum).

post, *prep. gov. acc.*, after, behind.

post·ea, *adv.*, after that, afterwards.

post-erus, -era, -erum, *adj.*, next, following.

prae·ceps, ·cip-itis, *adj.*, headlong, in headlong flight (prae, before ; caput, the head).

prae·cep-s,·cip-ītis, *adj.*, steep, precipitous (prae, caput, head foremost).

prae·clud-o, -ere, ·clus-i, ·clus-um, *v.a.* 3, I close in front, I block (prae : claudo, I shut).

praed-a, -ae, *f.*, booty, plunder.

prae·dic-o, *v.a.* 1, I declare, I announce.

praed-or, *v. dep.* 1, I plunder.

praefect-us, -i, *m.*, a prefect, a commander.

prae·fic-io, -ere, ·fēc-i, ·fect-um, *v.a.* 3, I place over, I appoint to the command of (prae, before ; facio, I make).

prae·miss-us, *from* praemitto.

prae·mitt-o, -ere, ·mīs-i, ·miss-um, *v.a.* 3, I send forward *or* in advance.

praesid-ium, -ii, *n.*, a protecting force, a garrison.

prae·st-o, -are, ·stĭt-i, ·stĭt-um, *v.a.* 1, I show, I perform, *v.n.*, I am superior.

prae·sum, ·esse, ·fui, *v.n.*, I am over, I rule.

praeter, *prep. gov. acc.*, except, besides.

praeterea, *adv.*, besides, more-over.

prěm-o, -ere, press-i, press-um, *v.a.* 3, I press hard, I harass.

pridĭe, adv., on the day before.

primo, *adv.*, at first, in the first place.

prīm-us, -a, -um, *adj.*, the first.

princ-eps, ·ĭpis, *m.*, a chieftain, a leading man.

pri-or, -us, *comp. adj.*, former, previous.

pris-tīnus, -tĭna, -tĭnum, *adj.*, former.

pro, *prep. gov. abl.*, before, instead of, as, for.

prob-o, *v.a.* 1, I approve, I think highly of.

pro·cēd-o (succedo), *v.n.* 3, I go forwards, I advance.

prŏcul, *adv.*, at a distance, far off.

pro·d-o, -ere, ·dĭd-i, ·dĭt-um, *v.a.* 3, I give up, I surrender, I betray.

pro·duc-o (*see* subduco,) *v.a.* 3, I prolong.

proel-ium, -ii, *n.*, a battle.

proeli-or, *v. dep.* 1, I join battle, I fight.

pro·fect-us, *from* proficiscor.

pro·ficisc-or, -i, ·fect-us sum, *v. dep.* 3, I set out.

pro·grěd-ior, -i, ·gress-us sum, *v. dep.* 3, I go forward, I advance, I proceed.

pro·gress-us, *from* progredior.

pro·hib-eo, *v.a.* 2, I hinder, I prevent, I protect.

pro·jic-io, -ere, ·jēc-i, ·ject-um, *v.a.* 3, I throw, I throw forward.

promiss-us, -a, -um, *adj.*, long, hanging down.

pro·mitt-o, *v.a.* 3, I send forward, I promise (*see* mitto).

prope, *prep.*, near ; *adv.*, nearly.

pro·pell-o, -ere, ·pŭl-i, ·puls-um, *v.a.* 3, I propel, I drive forward, I push forward.

propius, *comp. adv.*, nearer, too near (prope, near).

propter, *prep. gov. acc.*, on account of, because of.

pro·pugn-o, *v.n.* 1, I go forth to fight, I make sallies.

pro·sequ-or, *v. dep.* 3, I follow after, I pursue (*see* sequor).

prospect-us, -ūs, *m.*, sight.

protínus, *adv.*, forthwith, immediately.

pro·vect-us, *from* proveho.

pro·veh-o, -ere, ·vex-i, ·vect-um, *v.a.* 3, I carry forwards, I carry along.

pro·vid-eo (*see* video), *v.a.* 2, I foresee, I provide, I furnish.

proxĭm-us, -a, -um, *superl. adj.*, nearest, next.

Publ-ius, -ii, *m.*, Publius.

pugn-a, -ae, *f.*, a fight, a battle.

pugn-o, *v.a.* 1, I fight.

pulv-is, -ĕris, *m.*, dust.

put-o, *v.a.* 1, I think, I consider.

Q.=Quint-us, -i, *m.*, Quintus.

qua, *adv.*, in which place, where, wherever.

quadraginta, *num. adj. indecl.*, forty.

quaest-or, -ōris, *m.*, a quaestor.

quam, *adv.*, than.

quant-us, -a, -um, *adj.*, how great, how much.

quart-us, -a, -um, *adj.*, the fourth.

quattuor, *num. adj. indecl.*, four.

-que, *conj.*, and.

quĕr-or, -i, quest-us sum, *v. dep.* 3, I complain.

qui, quae, quod, *rel. pron.*, who, which, that.

qui·cumque, quae·cumque, quod·cumque, *rel. pron.*, whoever, whatever.

qui·dam, quae·dam, quod·dam, *indef. pron.*, some, certain.

quingent-i, -ae, *num. adj.*, five hundred.

quinque, *num. adj. indecl.*, five.

quin-tus, -ta, -tum, *num. adj.*, fifth.

Quintus, -i, *m.*, Quintus.

quis, quae, quid, *pron. interrog.*, who ? what ?

quis·quam, quae·quam, quic·quam *or* quid·quam, *pron. indef.*, any (person or thing).

quis·que, quae·que, quod·que, *adj. pron. indef.*, each, every.

quò, *adv.*, whither, where, in order that.

quo·ad, *adv.*, till, until.

quod, *conj.*, that, because that, inasmuch as.

quotidi-ānus, -āna, -ānum, *adj.*, daily.

quotidie, *adv.*, daily.

quum, *adv.*, when ; *conj.*, since, as, although.

rad-o, -ere, **ras**-i, **ras**-um, *v.a.* 3, I shave.

rar-us, -a, -um, *adj.*, dispersed here and there.

rebell-io, -iōnis, *f.*, a revolt.

recept-us, -ūs, *m.*, a retreat (recipio).

recipere se, to betake one's self, to recover one's self.

re·cip-io, -ere, **·cēp**-i, **·cept**-um, *v.a.* 3, I take back, I receive.

red·eo, **·ire**, **·īv**-i *or* **·i**-i, **·it**-um, *v.n. irreg.*, I go back, I return.

rĕdĭt-us, -ūs, *m.*, a returning, a return (redeo, I return).

re·duc-o, -ere, **·dux**-i, **·duct**-um, *v.a.* 3, I lead back.

refect-us, *from* reficio.

re·fĕr-o, **·re**, **re·ttŭl**-i, **re·lāt**-um, *v.a. irreg.*, I bring back, I carry back, I relate.

reficiend-as, *from* reficio.

re·fic-io, -ere, **·fēc**-i, **·fect**-um, *v.a.* 3, I repair.

reg-io, -iōnis, *f.*, a territory, a region.

regn-um, -i, *n.*, supreme power, a kingdom.

re·jic-io, -ere, **·jēc**-i, **·ject**-um, *v a.* 3, I throw back.

relict-us, *from* relinquo.

re·linqu-o, -ere, **·līqu**-i, **·lict**-um, *v.a.* 3, I leave.

rĕlĭqu-us, -a, -um, *adj.*, left, remaining.

re·man-eo, -ere, **-si** (no supine), *v.n.* 2, I remain behind.

rem·ĭg-o, *v.n.* 1, I row (remus, an oar).

re·migr-o (no perf. or supine), *v.n.* 1, I depart back, I return.

remiss-us, *part. perf. pass.* (remitto), mild, not severe.

re·mitt-o, -ere, **·mīs**-i, **·miss**-um, *v.a.* 3, I send back.

re·mŏv-eo, -ere, -i, **·mōt**-um, *v.a.* 2, I remove, I withdraw.

rēm-us, -i, *m.*, an oar.

re·nunti-o, *v.a.* 1, I bring back work, I report.

re·pell-o, -ere, **·pŭl**-i, **·puls**-um, *v.a.* 3, I drive back, I repulse.

repente, *adv.*, suddenly.

repentīn-us, -a, -um, *adj.*, sudden, unexpected.

re·pĕr-io, -ire, **rep·per**-i, **re·pert**-um, *v.a.* 4, I find out, I discover.

repert-us, *from* reperio.

report-o, *v.a.* 1, I carry back.

re-s, -i, *f.*, a thing, an affair, a circumstance.

re·sist-o, -ere, **·stit**-i (no supine), *v.n.* 3, I withstand, I halt.

res·publica, rei·publicae, *f.*, the commonwealth.

re·vert-or, -i, ·vers-us sum, *v. dep.* 3, I return.

re·voc-o, *v.a.* 1, I call back, I recall.

rex, rēg-is, *m.*, a king.

rip-a, -ae, *f.*, a bank.

Rom-a, -ae, *f.*, Rome.

Rōmān-us, -a, -um, *adj.*, Roman.

rot-a, -ae, *f.*, a wheel.

Ruf-us, -i, *m.*, Rufus.

rursus, *adv.*, back again, again.

sagitt-a, -ae, *f.*, an arrow.

satis, *adv.*, sufficiently, enough.

scaph-a, -ae, *f.*, a boat.

scrīb-o, -ere, scrips-i, script-um, *v.a.* 1, I write.

se (*or* sese), *reflex. pron., sing. and pl.*, himself, herself, itself, themselves.

secum, with himself (*cum is written after and joined to pers. pron.*).

secund-us, -a, -um, *adj.*, favourable, second.

secut-us, *from* sequor.

sed, *conj.*, but.

Segon-ax, -ācis, *m.*, Segonax.

Segontĭăc-i, ·orum, *m. pl.*, the Segontiaci.

sēmĭt-a, -ae, *f.*, a path.

senāt-us, -ūs, *m.*, the Senate.

septem. *num. adj. indecl.*, seven.

septentri-o, -ōnis (*most frequently pl.*), *m.*, the north.

sept-īmus, -īma, -ĭmum, *num. adj.*, seventh.

septingent-i, -ae, -a, *num. adj.*, seven hundred.

sĕqu-or, -i, sequut-us sum *or* secut-us sum, *v. dep.* 3, I follow.

sĕr-o, -ere, sēv-i, săt-um, *v.a.* 3, I sow.

serv-o, *v.a.* 1, I keep, I watch.

sese. *See* se.

si, *conj.*, if.

sic, *adv.*, so, thus. sicuti, to such a degree that (*see* ut).

sign-um, -i, *n.*, a signal, a (military) standard.

silv-a, -ae, *f.*, a wood.

silv-estris, -estre, *adj.*, woody (silva).

sĭmul, *adv.*, together, at once, at the same time.

simul atque, as soon as.

sine, *prep. gov. abl.*, without.

singulār-is, -e, *adj.*, single, solitary.

singul-i, -ae, -a, *num. distrib adj.*, separate, single, each.

sinistr-a, -ae, *f.*, the left hand.

sol, sol-is, *m.*, the sun.

sol-eo, -ēre, ĭtus sum, *semi-dep.*
2, I am wont, I am accus-
tomed.

solĭt-us, -a, -um, *adj.*, usual,
ordinary (soleo, I am accustomed).

sol-us, -a, -um, *adj.*, alone, only.

solv-o, -ere, -i, solut-um, *v.a.* 3,
I loosen (se, apart ; luo, I
loosen).

spat-ium, -ii, *n.*, space, distance,
interval of time.

speci-es, -ēi, *f.*, an appearance.

spect-o, *v.a.* 1, I look at *or*
towards.

speculator-ius, -ia, -ium, *adj.*,
pertaining to a spy *or* scout.

spe-s, -i, *f.*, hope, expectation.

stabil-ĭtas, -itatis, *f.*, steadiness
(stabilis, steady).

statim, *adv.*, immediately.

stat-io, -iōnis, *f.*, a station, an
outpost.

stătŭ-o, -ere, -i, stătūt-um, *v.a.*
3, I decide, I determine.

strepĭt-us, -ūs, *m.*, a noise.

stud-ium, -ii, *n.*, eagerness,
energy.

sub, *prep. gov. abl. and acc.*,
under, below, near, during.

sub·dūc-o, -ere, ·dux-i, ·duct-
um, *v.a.* 3, I draw ashore

(sub, from below ; duco, I
draw).

subĭto, *adv.*, suddenly.

sub·jĭc-io, -ere, ·jec-i, ·ject-um,
v.a. 3, I throw under, I place
near.

sub·ministr-o, *v.a.* 1, I supply,
I furnish.

sub·mitt-o, *v.a.* 3, I send, I
despatch (*see* mitto).

sub·sĕqu-or, *v. dep.* 3, I follow
close after, I follow in close
pursuit.

subsid-ium, -ii, *n.*, aid, assistance, a support.

sub·sist-o, -ere, ·stĭt-i, ·stĭt-um,
v.n. 3, I hold out.

sub·sum, ·esse, ·fui, *v.n.*, I am
near, I am at hand.

suc·cēd-o, -ere, ·cess-i, ·cess-um,
v.n. 3, I go in the place of,
I succeed (sub ; cedo, I go).

suc·cīd-o, -ere, -i, ·cis-um, *v.a.* 3,
I cut down (sub; caedo, I cut).

sud-es, -is, *f.*, a stake.

Sulpic-ius, -ii, *m.*, Sulpicius.

sum, esse, fu-i, *v.n. irreg.*, I am.

summ-a, -ae, *f.*, the whole, the
chief.

sum·mŏv-eo, -ere, ·mōv-i, ·mōt-
um, *v.a.* 2, I drive away
(sub, from beneath ; moveo,
I move).

summ-us, -a, -um, *superl. adj.*, highest, greatest, very great (*superl.* of superus).

superat-us, *from* supero.

super-ior, -ius, *adj.*, higher, upper, former, superior (*comp.* of superus).

super-o, *v.a.* 1, I overcome, I subdue, I conquer.

super·sum, ·esse, ·fui, *v.n.*, I remain, I am left.

supplicat-io, -iōnis, *f.*, a thanksgiving.

suspic-io, -iōnis, *f.*, mistrust, suspicion.

suspĭc-or, *v. dep.* 1, I mistrust, I suspect.

sus·tin-eo, -ere, -ui, ·tent-um, *v.a.* 2, I support, I check.

sustul-erant, *from* tollo.

su-us, -a, -um, *poss. pron.*, his own, her own, its own.

tale-a, -ae, *f.*, a rod, a bar.

tamen, *adv.*, nevertheless, yet.

Tamĕs-is, -is, *m.*, the Thames.

tandem, *adv.*, at length, at last.

tant-us, -a, -um, *adj.*, so much, so great.

Taximăgul-us, -i, *m.*, Taximagulus.

tĕg-o, -ere, **tex**-i, **tect**-um, *v.a.* 3, I cover.

tel-um, -i, *n.*, a weapon, a javelin.

tem-o, -ōnis, *m.*, the pole (of a carriage).

temperat-ior, -ius, *comp. adj.*, more temperate, milder.

tempes-tas, -tātis, *f.*, a time, a season, a storm.

temp-us, ŏris, *n.*, time, season.

ten-eo, *v.a.* 2, I hold, I detain, I keep.

terg-um, -i, *n.*, the back.

terr-or, -ōris, *m.*, alarm, terror.

ter·tius, -tia, -tium, *adj.*, the third.

test-ūdo, -ūdĭnis, *f.*, a covering, a shed.

tim-or, -ōris, *m.*, fear, terror.

toll-o, -ere, **sus·tul**-i, **sub·lat**-um, *v.a.* 3, I lift up, I carry away.

torment-um, -i, *n.*, a military engine.

tot, *num. adj. indecl.*, so many,

tot-us, -a, -um, *adj.*, the whole (*gen.*, totīus ; *dat.*, toti).

traject-us, -ūs, *m.*, a crossing, passage.

tranquillit-as, -ātis, *f.*, calmness, a calm.

trans·eo, -ire, ·iv-i *or* ·i-i, ·it-um, *v.a. irreg.*, I go across, I cross over.

trans·miss-us -ūs, *m.*, a passage (across the sea), (trans, across; mitto, I send).

transport-o, *v.a.* 1, I carry over, I transport.

Trebon-ius, -ii, *m.*, Trebonius.

tre·cent-i, -ae, -a, *num. adj.*, three hundred.

tres, tria (*gen.*, trium), *num. adj.*, three.

Trēvir-i, -orum, *m.*, the Treviri.

trib-ūnus, -ūni, *m.*, a tribune.

triginta, *num. adj. indecl.*, thirty.

Trinobant-es, -um, *m. pl.*, the Trinobantes.

tripartīto, *adv.*, in three divisions.

triquetr-us, -a, -um, *adj.*, triangular.

tu-eor, -eri, -ītus sum, *v. dep.*, 2, I protect, I defend.

tul erunt, *from* fero.

tul-it, *from* fero.

tum, *adv.*, then.

turm-a, -ae, *f.*, a troop, a squadron.

ubi, *adv.*, when, where.

ull-us, -a, -um, *adj.*, any.

ulter-ior, -ius, *comp. adj.*, further.

una, *adv.*, at one and the same time, together.

unde, *adv.*, whence.

undĭque, *adv.*, from all parts.

unĭvers-us, -a, -um, *adj.*, all together, the whole.

unquam, *adv.*, at any time, ever.

un-us, -a, -um, *adj.*, one.

u-sus, -sūs, *m.*, use, experience (utor).

ut (*or* uti), *adv. as conj.*, that, so that, in order that.

uter·que, utră·que, utrum·que, *pron. adj.*, both, each; as *subst. pl.*, both sides.

ut-or, -i, us-us sum, *v. dep.* 3, I use, I employ (with *abl.*).

vad-um, -i, *n.*, a shallow.

vag-or, *v. dep.* 1, I wander.

vall-um, -i, *n.*, a rampart.

vast-o, *v.a.* 1, I lay waste, I devastate, I plunder.

vectīg-al, -ālis, *n.*, a tax, tribute.

vector-ius, -ia, -ium, *adj.*, for carrying.

Vĕnĕt-ĭcus, -ĭca, -ĭcum, *adj.*, of *or* belonging to the Veneti.

vĕn-io, -ire, vēn-i, vent-um, *v.a.* 4, I come.

ventĭt-o, *v.n. intens.* 1, I keep coming.

vent-us, -i, *m.*, wind.

verg-o, -ere (*no perf. or supine*),
v.n. 3, I lie, I am situated.

vero, *conj.*, but, indeed, however.

vert-o, -ere, -i, vers-um, *v.a.* 3,
I turn.

vest-io, *v.a.* 4, I clothe.

vĕt-o, -are, -ui, -ĭtum, *v.a.* 1, I
forbid.

vĕt-us, ĕris, *adj.*, old.

vi-a, -ae, *f.*, a way, a road.

vicies, *adv.*, twenty times.

vĭd-eo, -ere, vīd-i, vīs-um, *v.a.*
2, I see ; *pass.*, I seem.

vigil-ia, -iae, *f.*, a watch.

viginti, *num. adj. indecl.*,
twenty.

vinc-ulum, -uli, *n.*, a chain, *a*
fetter (vincio, I bind).

vir-tus, -tūtis, *f.*, courage.

vis (*pl.*, vir-es, -ium), *f.*,
strength, violence.

vis-us. *See* video.

vit-o, *v.a.* 1, I avoid.

vitr-um, -i, *n.*, woad.

viv-o, -ere, vix-i, vict-um, *v.n.* 3,
I live.

voc-o, *v.a.* 1, I call.

vol-o, vel-le, volu-i, *v. irreg.*, I
am willing, I wish.

volupt-as, -ātis, *f.*, pleasure.

Volusēn-us, -i, *m.*, Volusenus.

vuln-us, -ĕris, *n.*, a wound.

vult-is, *from* volo.

EXERCISES.

Usual order of words in a simple sentence :—

1. Subject with extensions.
2. Adverbs or other extensions of Predicate.
3. Indirect Object.
4. Direct Object.
5. Predicate.

I.

RULES TO BE LEARNT.

(1) A verb agrees with the subject of the sentence in **gender, number**, and **person**.
(2) Adjectives agree with nouns in **gender, number**, and **case**.
(3) Transitive verbs usually take an **accusative** of the object.

1. (It) is now summer.
2. Of our enemies.
3. We are setting out.
4. For all the Britons.
5. In our wars.
6. We shall supply help.
7. Our enemies determined to set out.

II.

RULE.—Certain prepositions require the **accusative** case : **ante, apud, ad, circiter, contra, in** (into), **ob, per, post, praeter, prope, propter.**

1. We know the place.
2. He knew that place.
3. They are unknown to Caesar.
4. No one except you was known to me.
5. Except Caesar, no one set out.
6. The traders know the sea coast.

III.

RULE.—Certain prepositions require the **ablative** case : as **ab, cum, de, ex, in** (in), **pro, sine, sub** (*rest under*).

1. He set out with the traders.
2. We shall set out in a ship.
3. He wishes to approach the island.
4. Caesar wishes to send forward his forces.
5. I have been sent forward to the island with all the ships.
6. All the ships were in the harbour.

IV.

RULE.—Certain verbs require a **dative** case of the object : **adpropinquo, desum, ignosco, impero, noceo, objicio, obtempero, occurro, praesum, pareo, resisto.**

1. We shall obey the Romans.
2. The traders obeyed Caesar.

3. The hostages would have obeyed the lieutenant.
4. The inhabitants will make a fleet.
5. The ships will come to the war.
6. The lieutenant ordered me to come.

V.

RULE.—A **point** of time (time '*when*') is expressed by the **ablative** case; **duration** of time (time '*how long*') by the **accusative**.

1. Caesar sent the ships home.
2. On that day the fleet will return.
3. The king is not faithful to the Romans.
4. His courage does not seem to be great.
5. The enemy will not dare to approach the island.

VI.

1. Caesar wishes to prepare ships.
2. Caesar's plan is known to the enemy.
3. In the fifth year war was made.
4. The season of the year is not suitable for war.
5. We dare not tarry in this place.
6. Part of the enemy tarried in this place on account of the season of the year.

VII.

RULE.—Write **mecum, tecum, secum, nobiscum, vobiscum, quocum, quibuscum** for cum me, cum te, etc.

1. He had with him eighty ships.

2. They held the harbour for eighteen days.
3. On the fifth day the ships were seen.
4. He tarried with me eight days.
5. On the fifth day he will return with you.
6. The ships were detained by the wind eighteen days.

VIII.

Rule.—When 'him,' 'his,' 'them,' 'their,' etc., mean the same person or persons as the subject of the sentence, translate by the proper case of **se** and **suus**.

1. He sends his cavalry to the war.
2. Caesar sent his ambassador to the king.
3. Caesar ordered his soldiers to follow him (*that is*, Caesar).
4. The lieutenants had eight soldiers with them.
5. The Romans reached Britain with their ships.
6. Caesar had eighteen ships with him.
7. The Romans embarked upon their ships.

IX.

Rule.—When 'him,' 'his,' 'them,' 'their,' etc., do **not** mean the same person as the subject of the sentence, but refer to someone else mentioned before, use the proper case of 'is,' 'ea,' 'id.' **His** = ' of him ' = **ejus**. **Their** = ' of them ' = **eorum**.

1. His cavalry (*pl.*) was sent.
2. The place seems to them to be suitable.

3. Caesar assembled them.
4. Their ships have been seen.
5. The soldiers followed him (*that is*, Caesar).
6. For five days Caesar was waiting-for them.

X.

RULE.—Several verbs require an **ablative** case, as **utor, fungor** (I perform), **fruor** (I enjoy), **vescor** (I eat).

1. The Romans use ships in battle.
2. We shall not use the cavalry.
3. Caesar will use a suitable place for (*ad*) the battle.
4. The ships were drawn up on the shore.
5. He gave them (*dative*) the signal.
6. We do not use ships.

XI.

RULE.—Transitive verbs in the passive voice take an **ablative** case to express the **instrument** (the thing *by which*).

1. The ships are held back by the waves (*fluctus, -us*).
2. The sea is shut in by the mountain.
3. The soldier hurls the javelin with his hand.
4. The weight of the armour (*arma, pl.*) impedes the soldiers.
5. The soldiers are impeded by the weight of the armour.
6. They are not accustomed to use heavy armour.

XII.

RULE.—Transitive verbs in the passive voice take **a** or **ab** with the **ablative** case to express the **agent** (the person *by whom*). **A** is used before words commencing with a consonant, **ab** before words commencing with a vowel.

1. Our soldiers had been terrified by the appearance of the barbarians.
2. Our soldiers will not be terrified by the enemy (*pl.*).
3. The enemy (*pl.*) are terrified by this kind of warfare.
4. The ships are being propelled by oars.
5. The soldiers were being led (*ducere*) by Caesar.
6. The ships had been drawn up by the soldiers.
7. The signal had been given by Caesar.

XIII.

RULE.—An **ablative** case may combine with a **participle** to express the **time, cause, instrument**, or **manner** of the action of the principal verb in the sentence, as **Navibus factis**, Caesar in Britanniam transiit. We usually express the same thing in English by a complete sentence beginning with 'when,' 'while,' 'if,' etc. This construction is called **ablative absolute**.

1. While the soldiers were hesitating, he leaped down.
2. When the enemy had been seen, the soldiers returned to the ships.
3. If the eagle is surrendered, I shall not return.

4. If the soldiers hesitate, the eagle will be surrendered.
5. The signal having been given, the soldiers leaped down from the ship.
6. The standard-bearer will throw himself into the sea.
7. With Caesar (as) our general, we shall not fear disgrace.

XIV.

RULE.—The English infinitive expresses a **purpose**, as He came *to see* the games. In Latin a purpose is expressed by **ut** (=in order that) with **pres.** or **imperf. subjunctive**, as vēnit **ut** ludos videret. The **pres. subj.** is used after the **present, fut. simple, perfect** (with ' *have* '), **fut. perfect** in the principal sentence. The **imperf. subj.** is used after the **imperfect, perfect** (without ' *have* '), and **pluperfect** in the principal sentence.

1. He urges his horse, that he may see the enemy.
2. He urged his horse, that he might pursue the enemy.
3. He goes out to see (*purpose*) the enemy.
4. We shall have gone out to see the place.
5. We have gone out to see the horses.
6. We are going out to see the ships.

XV. (RECAPITULATORY).

1. The enemy was seen by Caesar.

2. When the ships are filled (*abl. abs.*), we shall make an attack.

3. The horses were terrified by the attack.

4. Caesar will use the ships.

5. If the ships follow (*abl. abs.*), we shall capture the island.

6. His horses were captured.

7. Having captured the horses (*abl. abs.*), he will return.

8. Caesar followed the enemy, that he might put them to flight (*fugare*).

XVI.

RULE.—Verbs meaning '**to say**,' '**to tell**,' '**to inform**,' '**to promise**,' or with any meaning implying '**speech**,' require the subject **of** the clause that follows to be in the **accusative case**, and the predicate in the **infinitive mood**. In English after these words we insert '**that**,' which is untranslated in Latin, as, He says that Caesar has come=Dicit Caesarem venisse.

1. He says that the enemy have sent ambassadors.

2. He promises to come [that he will come].

3. They say that the ambassadors have come.

4. Caesar promised to send [that he would send] help.

5. The ambassadors say that they were thrown into chains.

6. We promise to come [that we will come] with the ambassadors.

N.B.—Verbs of '*promising*' require a fut. infinitive and the accusative of the pronoun.

XVII.

RULE.—Same as preceding exercise.

1. Caesar says that he pardons the soldiers [Rule of Ex. iv.].
2. Caesar promises to pardon the soldiers.
3. The enemy promised to send hostages.
4. Caesar says that the Britons made war without cause.
5. He promises that he will not make war without cause.
6. Having sent ambassadors (*abl. abs.*), Caesar seeks peace.

XVIII.

RULE.—A Relative Pronoun is put in the same **gender, number,** and **person** as its antecedent; but its case is determined by its use in its own sentence.

1. The ships which were approaching Britain, were seen from the camp [Rule of Ex. iv.].
2. A storm arose, which filled the ships with water.
3. This is the island which Caesar has conquered.
4. I see the ships, which are coming into harbour.
5. The enemies, whom Caesar has subdued, are many.
6. I have seen the hostages, who were given to us.

XIX.

RULE.—The **Infinitive Mood** of a verb is really a **Verbal Noun** in the neuter gender, of which the gerunds are the

D

oblique cases ; as **navigare** = sailing.   Nom. and acc., **navigare** ; acc. after prepositions, **navigandum** ; gen., **navigandi** ; dat., **navigando** ; abl., **navigando**.

1. Sailing is not easy (*facil-is, -e*).
2. I love (*amare*) sailing.
3. These ships are useful (for use) for (*ad*) sailing.
4. We have come for the sake of (*causâ*) wintering.
5. I had an opportunity of sailing.
6. They came into Britain by sailing.
7. This place is useful for (*ad*) wintering.

XX. (RECAPITULATORY).

1. Caesar determines to come.
2. An opportunity of crossing will be given (xix.).
3. The camp, that Caesar made, was useless for wintering (xix.).
4. Caesar says that he will come after the battle (xvi.).
5. When the Britons are subdued (xiii.) we shall cross over.
6. He crosses the sea to wage war with the Britons (xiv.).

XXI.

RULE.—Verbs relating to the mind or the senses may take an **accusative** with the **infinitive** after them : such verbs are **to see, to feel, to know, to hear, to think, to believe**, etc.

1. Caesar knows that the lieutenants have come.

2. I suspect that hostages will be given.
3. I think that these (things) will be useful (for use) to us.
4. Caesar thinks that the lieutenants are collecting corn.
5. Caesar thinks that corn is being collected.
6. I think that twelve ships were lost.
7. I suspect that you know all our plans.

XXII. (RECAPITULATORY).

1. He promises *to send* other ships (xvi.).
2. I suspect that he has sent twelve ships (xxi.).
3. The lieutenants announce that the ships have come.
4. This is the legion that Caesar sent *to forage* (use supine in -um).
5. Caesar used three legions *for foraging* (*ad* with *acc.* of gerund).
6. The enemy's design was known to Caesar.
7. Caesar orders hostages to be given to him.
8. It is announced to Caesar that three legions have been seen.
9. The general orders three legions *to set out* with him (xiv.).
10. Caesar suspected the design of the enemy from (*ex*) the dust that he saw in that direction (*pars*).
11. Their design of foraging was known to Caesar.

12. Three legions have been sent *to forage* (use supine in -um).

XXIII.

Quum (=when) takes either **indicative** or **subjunctive**. It takes *indicative* if **simple time** is expressed; *subjunctive*, to denote **thought**; whether it be **cause** (=since), **succession** (=when), **contrast** (='although' or 'whereas').

1. When Caesar had ascertained this, he ordered the ambassadors to remain.
2. When they had laid down their arms, they followed the general.
3. When Caesar had come into the camp, he ordered the soldiers to reap the corn.
4. When the cavalry had surrounded the camp, the legion was thrown into confusion.
5. Caesar suspects that the enemy will come by night.
6. The general ascertains that the cavalry have laid down their arms.

XXIV.

RULE.—Same as preceding exercise.

1. The noise of the wheels frightens our horses.
2. When the charioteers had leaped down from (their) chariots, they fought on foot.
3. When Caesar had ridden through (*perequitare*) the line (*acies*) he ordered the cavalry to advance (*procedere*).

4. When they see the cavalry (*simple time*), they leap down from the chariots.
5. The general rides through the line, that he may encourage (*hortari*) the soldiers.
6. When the general has been killed (*simple time*), the soldiers lay down their arms.

XXV.

RULE.—'That' after '**so**,' '**such**,' '**so great**,' etc., is expressed in Latin by **ut** with the **subjunctive**; **ut** then introduces a **consequence**. The rule for the sequence of tenses is the same as in Ex. xiv.

1. So great (*tantus*) is the noise of the wheels that it frightens our horses.
2. The general is so (*tam*) skilful (*perīt-us, -a, -um*) that he conquers the enemy.
3. The place is so steep that we cannot check the horses.
4. They are so skilful that they can turn their horses in a very small space.
5. The general's horse is so swift (*incitatus*) that it is checked with difficulty (*aegre*).
6. This kind of fighting (*pugna*) is so new (*novus*) that it frightens our soldiers.

XXVI.

RULE.—The **Gerundive** is a **Verbal Adjective**. In translating the English verbal noun ending in -**ing** into Latin, if the verbal comes from a transitive verb, the **gerundive** is to be used instead of the gerund, and the following substantive, instead of being in the accusative case, is drawn into the case in which the gerund would have been, if it had been used. Thus you can translate 'the hope of making booty' by *spes praedandi* (intransitive) or by *spes praedae faciendae* (transitive), but NOT by *spes faciendi praedam*.

1. The hope of engaging in battle.
2. The fear of seeing the enemy.
3. The hope of gaining liberty.
4. An opportunity of restraining the soldiers.
5. Caesar has many opportunities of coming (*gerund*).
6. Many opportunities of seeing the battle were given to us.
7. The time is suitable for (*ad*) repairing (*reficere*) the ships.
8. We have hopes of seeing the army.
9. We shall have many opportunities of making booty.

XXVII.

RULE.—**Direct questions** are asked in Latin by means of **Interrogative Pronouns** and **Adverbs,** and by the particles **num, nonne** and **-ne. Num** expects the answer 'no,' **nonne,** 'yes,' and **-ne,** which must be attached to the first word of the sentence, simply asks for information. The chief interrogative pronouns are, **quis,** who? **ecquis,** any? **qualis,** of what kind? **quantus,** how great? **quot,** how many? and the chief interrogative adverbs, **ubi,** where? **unde,** whence? **quando,** when? **cur,** why?

1. Who is able to follow?
2. Have not ambassadors been sent by Caesar?
   [Yes.]

3. Have you seen the general? [No.]
4. Have you not seen the cavalry? [Yes.]
5. Are you able to come?
6. How many soldiers had Caesar? Don't you know?
7. How great is the army?
8. Do you think that Caesar will depart before the winter?
9. Who can escape danger?
10. When will you come?

XXVIII.

RULE.—See preceding exercise.

1. How great is the number of the hostages?
2. How many ships has Caesar?
3. Can they be brought to the island?
4. Do you not think that Caesar is a good (*bon-us, -a, -um*) general?
5. Do you think that the soldiers will fight without their general?
6. Has not the general set out for (*ad*) the army?

XXIX. (RECAPITULATORY).

1. Caesar tarried five days in the camp.
2. He ordered the legions to follow him.
3. What wind is blowing?
4. The time is unsuitable for (*ad*) making the harbour.
5. Ships were sent to defend the harbour.

6. Caesar sends the five legions which he had left in camp.

7. Did you not promise to come ?   [Yes.]

8. Have you heard (*audire*) that the general will furnish corn ?

9. Have you not had many opportunities of coming ?

XXX.

RULE.—The **gerundive** agreeing in **gender** and **number** with the subject of a sentence may combine with any part of the verb 'esse' to form the predicate.   This construction expresses *duty*, *fitness*, or *necessity*, as Virtus laudanda est, = Valour is to be praised = Valour ought to be praised = Valour must be praised.

1. The soldiers must be praised.

2. The island ought to be captured.

3. The Britons must be subdued.

4. Corn must be furnished for the troops.

5. The ships must be left in the harbour.

6. The course of the ships must be changed (*mutare*).

7. Caesar is to be praised on account of his courage.

XXXI.

RULE.—The gerundive takes a **dative** with it to denote the agent *by whom* instead of the ablative with *a* or *ab*.

1. The courage of the Britons is to be praised by the Romans.

2. The enemies must be subdued by us.

3. Labour must not be relaxed by us.

4. The plan of the general must be approved of by good soldiers.

5. Our ranks must not be broken by the enemy.

6. A time suitable for sailing must be sought by the general.

XXXII.

REMARK.—The **Gerundive** is **passive**. It is used to translate '*must*' or '*ought*' with an active verb in English by turning the sentence first into the Passive construction and then translating literally, thus: We must praise valour = Valour is to be praised by us = Virtus nobis laudanda est. Turn the following sentences in this way before translating.

1. You must praise the soldiers.

2. Caesar must furnish corn.

3. We must see the ships.

4. We must subdue the Britons.

5. We must praise the labours of the soldiers.

6. I must leave the island.

XXXIII.

RULE.—An **Indirect Question** is one that depends upon such verbs as **ask, doubt, know,** &c. **Interrogatives** introduce the indirect question (as in xxvii.), and the verb is in the **subjunctive mood**.

Rule for sequence of tenses same as in xiv.

Where are you? (Direct Question.) Ubi es?

I asked him where you were.   (Indirect Question.)   Rogavi eum ubi esses.

1. Where is the enemy?   [Direct Question.]
2. I will ask [*rogare*] where the enemy is.   [Indirect Question.]
3. Caesar did *not know* [*ignorare*] where the enemy was.
4. I ask you why (*cur*) you do not come.
5. I shall ascertain where Caesar is.
6. He will show me (*dat.*) where the enemy have encamped.
7. I asked the general how many legions he had.

XXXIV. (Recapitulatory).

1. The ships must be drawn up, and the camp must be fortified.
2. Ten days must be spent in this work.
3. How many days will you spend?
4. I will ask Caesar how many days he spent in repairing the ships.   [xxxiii.]
5. How great is the army?
6. The general replied (*respondēre*) that he had four thousand men.   [xvi.]
7. I asked the general how many days he had spent.
8. Did you not ascertain where the enemy had encamped?   [xxvii.]
9. Caesar ascertains that the Britons have lost thirty ships.   [xxi.]

XXXV. (Recapitulatory).

1. When the general had seen the enemy, [xxiii.] he commanded the soldiers to draw up the ships, [xvi.] and to fortify the camp.
2. He did not think that the enemy would come. [xxi.]
3. Nevertheless [*tamen*, second word in sentence] he left one legion to guard [= for a guard to] the camp.
4. And set out by night to meet Caesar. [xiv.]
5. When he had returned, he was asked where Caesar was. [xxxiii.]
6. He replied that Caesar had not been seen.

XXXVI.

RULE.—Verbs of **making**, **calling**, **thinking**, **believing**, &c., require the **Nom. Case** after them when they are in the Passive Voice : as Creatur Consul, = he is made consul : insula appellatur Mona, = the island is called Mona.

1. This island was called Britain.
2. The winter is thought to be very short.
3. A part of the legion was called a cohort.
4. One part of the year is called winter.
5. Caesar is made general.
6. He is thought to be the best general.
7. The king was called Cassivellaunus.

XXXVII. (Recapitulatory).

1. The nights are shorter in Britain than in Gaul.
2. The island is thought to be Britain.

3. Is all the island inhabited?   [No.]
4. Do not the inhabitants till the fields?   [Yes.]
5. The Belgae crossed over that they might make booty.   [xiv.]
6. The enemy will come *for the sake of* (*causâ* with gen. case) making booty.   [xxvi.]
7. After making booty [xiii.] the enemy will cross over.

XXXVIII. (RECAPITULATORY).

1. The Britons are said to use lead.
2. Is (there) not a large quantity of iron in Britain?   [Yes.]
3. There is such (*tant-us, -a, -um*) a quantity of iron in Britain, that the inhabitants use it for many purposes (*ad multas res*).   [xxv.]
4. Do the Britons use buildings?   [No.]
5. Do you not think that Britain is milder than Gaul?   [Yes.]
6. Why do you think that it is not lawful to use lead?

XXXIX. (RECAPITULATORY).

1. Corn is to be sown in the winter.   [xxx.]
2. Which is the most civilized people of Britain?
3. Have not very many men been killed in battle?   [Yes.]   [xxvii.]
4. How many men have you lost?   [xxvii.]
5. He asked how many men we had lost.   [xxxiii.]
6. He had an intention of sowing corn.   [xxvi.]
7. They go out to sow corn.   [xiv.]

XL.

RULE.—Instead of an **adverb** with the predicate, an **adjective** agreeing with the subject expressed or understood, may sometimes be used, as *incolumes redierunt* = they returned safely.

1. The enemies show themselves in scattered bands.
2. They did this unwillingly (*invitus* = unwilling).
3. They thoughtlessly (*imprudens*) make an attack.
4. Caesar returned safely to the camp.
5. The Britons vigorously break through our cavalry.
6. The Britons thoughtlessly encamped upon the hills.

XLI.

RULE.—**Causâ** (= for the sake of) with the **genitive** of the gerund of an intransitive verb, or with the **genitive** of a noun and a **gerundive** of a transitive verb agreeing with it, may be used to express a **purpose**, as, Caesar *pabulandi causâ* tres legiones misit = Caesar sent three legions to forage ; Caesar *hostium expellendorum causâ* legionem unam misit = Caesar sent one legion to dislodge the enemy.

1. Caesar sent five soldiers to forage.
2. They go into the fields to sow corn.
3. They go to till the fields.
4. Caesar will send soldiers to fortify the camp.
5. Caesar sent the legions into Gaul to winter.
6. Two legions were sent to make an attack.

XLII. (RECAPITULATORY).

1. Caesar orders the cavalry to cross the river.

2. An opportunity of following was not given. [xxvi.]
3. Having sent forward the cavalry, Caesar delays. [xiii.]
4. The soldiers were sent into the fields to reap the corn. [xiv.]
5. The bank was so exceedingly well fortified that the cavalry were not able to cross the river. [xxv.]

XLIII. (RECAPITULATORY).

1. All hope of making booty was laid aside. [xxvi.]
2. Caesar had sent two legions to lay waste the fields. [xli.]
3. Having dismissed (his) forces, Caesar returned to the city. [xiii. or xxiii.]
4. The Roman soldier unwillingly gives himself to flight. [xl.]
5. Caesar unwillingly suffered the legions to leave the camp. [xl.]
6. An opportunity of engaging with the enemy will be given. [xxvi.]

XLIV. (SEE EXERCISE XVI.)

RULE.—The **future** infinitive is used after the verbs '**to promise**,' '**to hope**,' '**to undertake**,' where in English we use the present infinitive, as, He hopes to come = sperat se venturum esse.

1. He promises to send ambassadors.
2. He promised to ask Caesar.
3. They have promised to send hostages.

4. He hopes (*sperare*) to see his father.
5. They hope to avoid death by flight.
6. We hope that the king will defend the **town**.

XLV.

RULE.—See preceding exercise.

1. Caesar promised to defend the soldiers
2. I hope Caesar will set out before the winter.
3. The soldiers hoped that Caesar would not leave the town.
4. Caesar had promised that he would not leave the town.
5. I hope that a large number of men will assemble.
6. The legions promised to surrender themselves to the enemy.

XLVI.

RULE.—When **ut** with subj. expresses a **purpose**, **ut** becomes **ne** when there is a **negative** in the sentence ; when **ut** with subj. denotes a consequence, if there be a **negative** in the sentence, **ut** remains and the negative is expressed by **non**. Observe the following variations :

	Purpose.		*Consequence.*
(*a*) **That…not**	(1) **ne**	(2) **ut … non.**
(*b*) **That nobody**	(1) **ne quis**	(2) **ut nemo.**
(*c*) **That nothing**	(1) **ne quid**	(2) **ut nihil.**
(*d*) **That never**	(1) **ne unquam**	(2) **ut nunquam.**

1. He commands the legions not to (*a* 1) attack the camp.

2. He orders that nobody (*b* 1) may come into the
   camp.

3. Caesar commands the legions not to (*a* 1) take
   prisoners.

4. I ask you not to (*a* 1) come before night.

5. I commanded the legions not to (*c* 1) plunder
   anything.

6. Cassivellaunus was so greatly moved by the revolt
   of the citizens, that he never (*d* 2) returned to
   the town.

7. He had received so many losses that he was not
   (*a* 2) able to pay tribute.

XLVII. (Recapitulatory).

1. Caesar orders the general to lead back [xiv.] the
   army.

2. The number of the soldiers is so great that the ships
   are not able to carry all.   [xxv. and xlvi.]

3. The harbour was so small that it was not able to
   receive all the ships.   [xxv. and xlvi.]

4. Have not the ships been repaired?   [Yes.]

5. After a storm follows a calm.

6. When the soldiers had repaired the ships, they
   decided to sail.

VOCABULARY.

(ENGLISH-LATIN.)

The Roman Numerals refer to the Exercises; the other Numerals to the Vocabularies.

able (to be), 3.
account of (on), 6.
accustomed ('to be), 10.
advance (to), 8.
after, 6.
all, 1.
anything, xlvi.
ambassador, 4.
announce (to), 22.
appearance, 12.
approach (to), 13.
arise (to), 18.
armour, 11.
arms, 11.
army, 19.
ascertain (to), 2.
ask (to), xxxiii.
assemble (to), 3.
attack (an), 15.
avoid (to), 44.

bank, 42.
barbarian, 5.
battle, 10.
be (to), 1.
before, 35.
Belgae, 28.
best, 30.
blow (to), 29.
bold, xl.
booty, 26.
break (to), 19.
bring to (to), 28.
Britain, 1.
Briton, 1.
building, 27.
by, 4.

Caesar, 1.
call (to), 22.
calm, 47.

forage (to), 22.
forces, 3.
fortify, 32.
four, 43.
frighten (to), 12.
from, 4.
furnish (to), 19.

gain (to), 23.
Gaul, 19.
general, 13.
give (to), 4.
go (to), 42.
go out (to), 24.
great, 5.
greatly, 3.
guard, 7.

hand, 11.
harbour, 2.
have (to), 5.
hear (to), xxix.
heavy, 11.
help, 1.
hesitate (to), 13.
hill, 8.
him, 17.
himself, 3.
his, 3.
hold (to), 7.
hold back (to), 7.
home, 5.
hope, 43.

horse, 11.
hostage, 4.
how great, 26.
how many, 26.
hurl (to), 11.

impede (to), 11.
in, 1.
inhabit, 37.
inhabitants, 3.
intention, 4.
into, 1.
iron, 38.
island, 3.

javelin, 9.

kill (to), 23.
kind, 2.
king, 5.
know (to), 2.
know (not to), 32.

labour, 30.
large, 5.
lawful, 38.
lay aside (to), 23.
lay down (to), 23.
lay waste (to), 43.
lead, 38.
lead (to), 42.
lead back (to), 26.
leap down (to), 13.

leave (to), 6.
legion, 13.
liberty, 26.
lieutenant, 4.
line, 27.
lose (to), 19.
loss, 46.
love (to), xix

make (to), 6.
man, 2.
many, 34.
me, 13.
meet (to), 14.
milder, 38.
mountain, 9.
move (to), 12.
move deeply (to), 12.

nevertheless, 1.
new, 22.
night, 18.
by night, 23.
nobody, xlvi.
noise, 24.
no one, 2.
not, 3.
now, 1.
number, 6.

oar, 12.
obey, 28.
on account of, 6.

one, 9.
opportunity, 6.
order (to), 4.
our, 1.

pardon (to), 17.
part, 1.
pay (to), 46.
peace, 16.
people, 39.
place, 2.
plan, 4.
plunder (to), 43.
praise (to), 30.
prepare (to), 6.
prisoner, 31.
promise (to), 5.
propel (to), 12.
provoke (to), 40.
purposes, 38.
pursue (to), 15.
put to flight (to), 15.

quantity, 3.

rank, 14.
reach (to), 8.
reap (to), 23.
receive (to), 33.
relax (to), 21.
remain (to), 22.
repair (to), 19.
reply (to), xxxiv.
restrain (to), 9.
return (to), 5.

revolt, 46.
ride through (to), 24.
river, 32.
Roman, 4.

safely, 28.
sail (to), 19.
say (to), 17.
sea, 9.
sea coast, 2.
season, 8.
see (to), 5.
seek (to), 17.
seem (to), 5.
seldom, 32.
send (to), 5.
send forward (to). 3.
set out (to), 1.
ship, 3.
shore, 9.
short, 3.
shorter, 3.
show (to), 26.
shut in (to), 9.
signal, 9.
small, 1.
so, 19.
so great, 13.
so many, 46.
soldier, 9.
sow (to), 39.
space, 25.
spend (to), 32.

standard bearer, 13.
steep, 25.
storm, 8.
subdue (to), 16.
suffer (to), 33.
suitable, 6.
summer, 1.
supply (to), 1.
surrender (to), 13.
surround (to), 23.
suspect (to), 21.
swift, 25.

take (to), 15.
tarry (to), 6.
ten, 31.
terrify (to), 12.
that (*conj.*), 13.
that (*dem.*), 2.
their, 3.
them, 17.
themselves, 3.
think (to), 36.
this, 2.
thirty, 27.
thousand, 7.
three, 29.
throw into (to), 13.
throw into confusion (to), 14.
till (to), 37.
town, 45.
trader, 2.
tribute, 46.

INDEX.

The Numbers refer to the Chapters.

96 INDEX.

semita, 43.
senatus, 28.
septem, 10.
septentrio, 37.
septimus, 22.
septingenti, 37.
sequor, 8.
sero, 39.
servo, 14.
seso, 44.
si, 24.
sic, 41.
sic uti, 41.
signum, 9.
silva, 23.
silvestris, 43.
simul, 15.
simul atque, 16.
sine, 17.
singularis, 14.
singuli, 46.
sinistra, 30.
sol, 18.
soleo, 25.
solitus, 12.
solus, 42.
solvo, 8.
spatium, 25.
species, 12.
specto, 36.
speculatorius, 15.
spes, 43.
stabilitas, 25.
statim, 16.
statio, 22.
statuo, 1.
strepitus, 24.
studium, 21.
sub, 30.
subduco, 19.
subito, 18.
subjicio, 36.

subministro, 1.
submitto, 15.
subsequor, 10.
subsidium, 15.
subsisto, 33.
subsum, 47.
succedo, 22.
succido, 32.
sudes, 42.
Sulpicius, 7.
sum, 1.
summa, 35.
summoveo, 12.
summus, 11.
superatus, 20.
superior, 6.
supero, 16.
supersum, 46.
supplicatio, 28.
suspicio, 22.
suspicor, 21.
sustineo, 25.
sustulerant, 18.
suus, 3.

talea, 38.
tamen, 1.
Tamesis, 35.
tandem, 29.
tantus, 13.
Taximagulus, 46.
tego, 42.
telum, 9.
temo, 25.
temperatior, 38.
tempestas, 8.
tempus, 6.
teneo, 7.
tergum, 6.
terror, 24.
tertius, 8.
testudo, 32.

timor, 25.
tollo, 9.
tormentum, 12.
tot, 46.
totus, 19.
trajectus, 3.
tranquillitas, 47.
transeo, 29.
transmissus, 36.
transporto, 19.
Trebonius, 41.
trecenti, 31.
tres, 29.
Treviri, 28.
tribunus, 9.
triginta, 27.
Trinobantes, 44.
tripartito, 33.
triquetrus, 36.
tueor, 29.
tulerunt, 45.
tulit, 25.
tum, 8.
turma, 24.

ubi, 12.
ullus, 18.
ulterior, 8.
una, 5.
unde, 18.
undique, 4.
universus, 13.
unquam, 41.
unus, 9.
usus, 3.
ut, 13.
uterque. 14.
utor, 10.

vadum, 14.
vagor, 43.
vallum, 45.

PRINTED IN GREAT BRITAIN BY ROBERT MACLEHOSE AND CO. LTD.
THE UNIVERSITY PRESS, GLASGOW